OBD II FAULT TABLES

KOTZIG PUBLISHING

© Kotzig Publishing, Inc., 2003
www.kotzigpublishing.com

Printed in Slovakia

ISBN 0-9715411-5-9

KOTZIG PUBLISHING

Disclaimer. This publication is being sold with no warranties of any kind, express or implied. This publication is intended for educational and informational purposes only, and should not be relied upon as a "how-to" guide in performing repairs, maintenance or modification of your vehicle. This publication is not endorsed by the manufacturer of your vehicle nor AST, DiabloSport or ToolRama, and there is no affiliation between the publisher and author and the manufacturer of your vehicle.

Modifications performed on your vehicle may limit or void your rights under any warranty provided by the manufacturer of your vehicle, and neither the publisher nor the author of this publication assume any responsibility in such event. Any warranty not provided herein, and any remedy which, but for this provision, might arise by implication or operation of law, is hereby excluded and disclaimed. The implied warranties of merchantability and of fitness for any particular purpose herein are expressly disclaimed.

No Liability For Damages, Injuries Or Incidental, Special Or Consequential Damages. Under no circumstances shall the publisher, author, or contributing author of this publication, or any other related party, be liable to purchaser or any other person for any damage to your vehicle, loss of use of your vehicle, or for personal injuries suffered by any person, or for any incidental, special or consequential damages, whether arising out of negligence, breach of warranty, breach of contract, or otherwise.

State Law. Some states do not allow limitations of implied warranties, or the exclusion or limitation of incidental, special or consequential damages, so the above limitations may not apply to you. In such states, liability shall be limited to the greatest extent permitted by applicable law.

Warning. Although the publisher and author have made every effort to ensure accuracy of all information contained in this publication, the reader should not attempt any modifications of his or her vehicle or computer codes without the assistance of a qualified and trained technician. Always obey state and federal laws, follow manufacturers' operating instructions and observe safety precautions. All information contained in the publication is for educational and informational purposes only and is not intended as a "how-to" guide.

Note. All trademarks are property of their individual owners.

LIST OF FAULT TABLES

This chapter is an excerpt from Peter David's previous book, OBDII Diagnostic Secrets Revealed.

It is an introduction to the anatomy of OBDII, describing the Diagnostic Connector, Protocols, Trouble Codes and Terminology.

If you are interested in learning more about the history, theory and principles of OBDII diagnostics, then Peter David's previous book is for you! To view its contents, please visit www.kotzigpublishing.com.

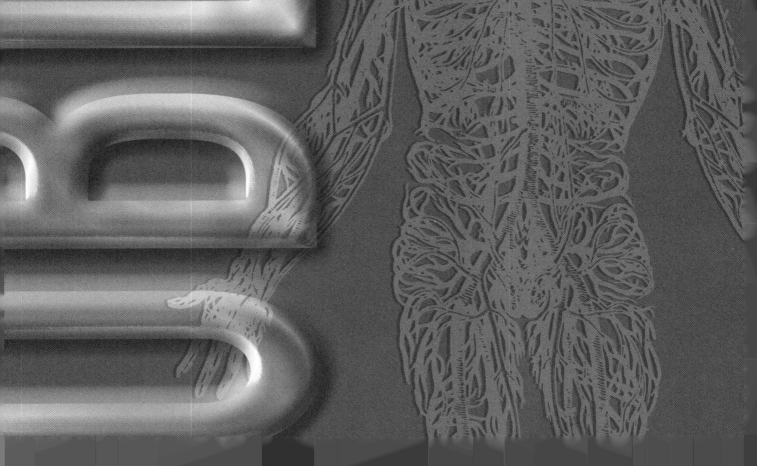

> The Anatomy of OBD II

Basics

As you just read in the History chapter, OBDII is not some basic concept that was just thrown together. It took years of development. Please remember, OBDII is not an Engine Management System. It is a set of rules and regulations that each manufacturer must follow in order to have their Engine Management System pass Federal Emissions. To best understand what OBDII is we must break it down into sections. When doctors are studying, they don't just study the body as a whole, they study part by part. In the end, all the parts come together. That is what we are doing here. OBDII must have all of the following parts to make up the standardization.

One centralized diagnostic connector with specific pins with assigned specific functions

The diagnostic connector (OBDII calls it the Diagnostic Link Connector - DLC) main function is to enable the diagnostic scan tool to communicate with OBDII compliant control units. The DLC must follow the standards set by SAE J1962. According to J1962, the DLC must have a centralized location in the vehicle. It must be within 16 inches of the steering wheel. The manufacturer can place the DLC in one of eight possible places predetermined by the EPA.

Each pin has its assigned definition. Assignment of many of the pins is still

---

The standard OBDII connector

Pin 1 - *Proprietary*

Pin 2 - *J1850 Bus+*

Pin 3 - *Proprietary*

Pin 4 - *Chassis Ground*

Pin 5 - *Signal Ground*

Pin 6 - *CAN High (J-2284)*

Pin 7 - *ISO 9141-2 (K Line)*

Pin 8 - *Proprietary*

Pin 9 - *Proprietary*

Pin 10 - *J1850 Bus-*

Pin 11 - *Proprietary*

Pin 12 - *Proprietary*

Pin 13 - *Proprietary*

Pin 14 - *CAN Low (J-2284)*

Pin 15 - *ISO 9141-2 (L Line)*

Pin 16 - *Battery Power*

left up to the manufacturer, but those pins are not meant to be used by OBDII compliant control units. They can be for Supplemental Restraint Systems (SRS), or Anti-Lock Brake Systems (ABS) to name just two.

You may have noticed the connector has its own power and ground source (pins 4, 5 are ground, pin 16 is power). This is so that a scan tool won't require an external power source. If you plug in a diagnostic scan tool, and it doesn't power up, first check pin 16 for power, and then pins 4 and 5 for a ground. You probably noticed

also these alphanumeric characters: J1850, CAN and ISO 9141-2. These are protocol standards developed by SAE and ISO. The manufacturers have their choice of these standards to use for their diagnostic communication.

Each standard has a specific pin to communicate on. For example, Ford products communicate on pins 2, and 10. GM products communicate on pin 2. Most Asian and European products communicate on pin 7, and some, also, on pin 15.

OBD II DIAGNOSTIC

Which protocol is used makes no difference to understanding OBDII. The message exchanged between the diagnostic tool and the control unit is always exactly the same, only the way it is transmitted differs.

 IN LAYMAN'S TERMS, one standardized connector, with one shape, in one location, makes it easier and cheaper for the repair shops. They don't need 20 different connectors or tools for 20 different vehicles. In addition, this saves time, since the repair shops won't have to hunt down the location of the connector to hook up the tool.

Standardized diagnostic communication protocols

As seen above, OBDII recognizes several different protocols. At this point, we only need to discuss three of them: J1850-VPW; J1850-PWM; and ISO9141, which directly affect all the vehicles in the United States.

All the control units in the vehicle are connected with a cable (called a diagnostic bus), creating a network. We can connect a Diagnostic Scan Tool to the diagnostic bus. The tool will send out a signal to the specific control unit to which it wants to communicate. The control unit will respond. Communication will continue until the tool terminates communication or the tool is disconnected.

For instance, the Diagnostic Scan Tool will ask the control unit "What are your faults?" The control unit will answer appropriately. With that simple communication exchange, we have just followed a protocol.

 IN LAYMAN'S TERMS, protocol is a set of rules that must be followed in order for a network to complete a communication.

Classification of a Protocol

SAE has defined three distinct protocol Classifications, Class A, Class B, and Class C.

Class A is the slowest of the three and can be as high as 10,000 bytes per second or 10Kb/s. The ISO 9141 standard uses the Class A protocol.

Class B is ten times faster and supports communication of data as high as 100Kb/s. The SAE J1850 Standard is a Class B protocol.

Class C supports communication performance as high as 1Mb/s. The most widely used vehicle-networking standard for Class C is Controller Area Network (CAN). Higher performance communication classifications from 1Mb/s to 10Mb/s are expected in the future. Classifications like Class D can be expected as bandwidth and performance needs go forward. With Class C, and the futuristic Class D protocols, we will be able to use fiber optics as cabling for the network.

J1850 PWM protocol

J1850 comes in two different flavors. The first is a high speed 41.6 Kb/s Pulse Width Modulation (PWM). Ford, Jaguar and Mazda use this. Ford was the first to use this type of communication. The communication uses two wires, pins 2 and 10 of the diagnostic connector.

J1850 VPW protocol

The other J1850 alternative is the 10.4 Kb/s Variable Pulse Width (VPW). Both General Motors (GM) and Chrysler use this protocol. It is very similar to Ford's protocol, but the communication is much slower. It uses one wire, pin 2 of the diagnostic connector.

ISO 9141 protocol

The third protocol is the ISO 9141, defined by the International Standard Organization (ISO). Most European, Asian, and some Chrysler vehicles use this standard.

It is not as complex as the J1850 standards. While the J1850 protocols require use of specialized communication microprocessors, ISO 9141 uses standard off-the-shelf serial communication chips.

 IN LAYMAN'S TERMS, OBDII uses a standardized diagnostic communication protocol, because the EPA wanted a standard way for repair shops to diagnose and repair vehicles properly. They wanted this without the expense of proprietary equipment.

For more intense description of the protocols, please refer to Chapter 4, Understanding OBDII Protocol.

OBD II DIAGNOSTIC

Malfunction Indication Lamp (MIL) Operation

When the engine management has detected an emission related problem, the Check Engine light will come on. OBDII calls the light a Malfunction Indicator Light (MIL). The MIL will typically display

the phrase "Service Engine Soon," "Check Engine" or "Check."

The MIL's purpose is to tell the driver of the vehicle there is a problem with the engine management system. If the MIL comes on, please don't panic. It is not life threatening. Your engine will not blow up. If the oil light or the overheat warning light comes on, then it is time to panic. The OBDII MIL is just telling the driver that there is a problem with the engine management system that will cause excessive emissions from the tailpipe or the evaporative fuel systems.

 IN LAYMAN'S TERMS, The MIL will come on if there is a problem with the system that manages the engine. Meaning, if a spark

plug gets fouled, or the gas cap comes off. Anything that allows excessive gas vapor to the atmosphere.

To check the function of the MIL: Turn the ignition to the run position (when all the lights come on in the dashboard), the MIL will illuminate. According to OBDII the light must come on for a period of time. Some manufacturers will have the MIL stay on, and others will come on then after a period of time it will turn off. If you start the engine, and all the conditions are met and no faults are found, the MIL will turn off.

The MIL will not necessarily come on when a fault first happens. The importance of the fault will determine when the MIL will come on. If the importance is listed as high, meaning if you have a gross petulant, then the MIL will come on immediately. The fault is listed as Active. Or, if the fault is a problem, but not enough to exceed the gross pollutant status, then the light will not come on, but will be placed in Stored status. In order for the fault to be listed as Active, it must happen on several occasions, called drive cycles. Typically a drive cycle is when a vehicle is started cold and driven to normal operating temperature (with coolant temperature below 122 F and the coolant and air temperature sensors within 11 degrees of one another). During this process all the on-board emission monitor tests must be completed.

Different vehicles have different engine sizes, and the drive cycle is slightly different for each. For further description of a drive cycle, please refer to the GM, Ford and Chrysler diagnostic tips section. On an average vehicle, if a fault is seen in 3 drive cycles then the MIL will come on. On the other hand, if the fault is not seen in 3 drive cycles, then the MIL will go out.

So, if the MIL comes on and goes out, don't worry. The fault remains stored in the PCM, and can be retrieved with a scan tool. As mentioned, there are two states that the fault can be in; Stored or Active. Stored is when the fault has been detected, but the MIL is not on, or was on and went out. Active is when the fault is present, and the MIL is on.

A Standardized set of Diagnostic Trouble Codes (DTC)

OBDII calls a fault a Diagnostic Trouble Code (DTC). A DTC is made up of a combination of 1 letter and 4 digits, as designated by SAE J2012. The figure below shows what each character means.

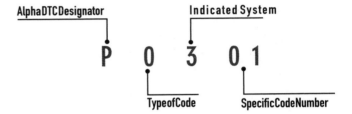

DTC Alpha Designator

As you can see, each character has a meaning. The first character is the DTC Alpha Designator. This letter identifies in which part of the vehicle the fault is found. The assignment of the letter (P, B, C, or U) is determined by the control unit being diagnosed. If two control units respond, the one with priority is listed. There can only be four letters found in this position:

P = Powertrain: these faults are related to the Engine, and Transmission

B = Body: faults that are related to the Body of the Vehicle (i.e. SRS, Instrument cluster)

C = Chassis: faults that are related to the Chassis of the Vehicle (i.e. ABS, Traction systems)

U = Network Communication: faults that are related to the CAN

Type of Code

The second character is the most controversial - it shows who defined the code:

Value 0 (commonly known as "P0" code) means it is a generic, publicly known SAE fault code (see Appendix A for a complete list of generic P0 fault codes).

Value 1 (commonly known as "P1" code) means it is a proprietary fault code, defined by the vehicle manufacturer (see appropriate chapters for a complete list of P1 fault codes).

Most scanners are unable to recognize the description or text of the P1 codes. However, Hellion by DiabloSport (www.eobd.com) is one of the few

that can recognize most of them. SAE made up the original DTC list, but the manufacturers complained that they had their own systems and each system was different. Mercedes has a completely different system than Honda, etc. They cannot use each other's codes, so the SAE made a provision to separate the standard codes (P0 codes) from manufacturer specific codes (P1 codes).

Indicated System

The third character is the Indicated System. This character is one of the least known, and most helpful. It will tell you the affected system, without even looking up the fault text. It helps to quickly identify the general area of the problem without knowing the exact description of the code. The numbers that are found here are as follows, if the number is:

1 = Faults that relate to the Air/Fuel Control Systems
2 = Faults related to the Fuel System (i.e. injectors)
3 = Faults that deal with Ignition System/Misfire
4 = Faults related to the Auxiliary Emission Controls (i.e. EGR, AIR, CAT, EVAP)
5 = Faults related to the Vehicle

Speed/Idle Control and Auxiliary Inputs
6 --7 = Transmission or Transaxle
8 = Transmission or Transaxle

Specific Code Number

The fourth and fifth characters are usually viewed together. These usually relate to the older OBDI fault code. OBDI DTCs are usually two digit faults. OBDII just took the two digit codes and put them on the end of the fault. This made it easier to distinguish the faults.

Now that we know what makes up the DTC, lets take the DTC P0301 as an example. Without even looking up the text, we have an idea of what the fault is. First, by the "P", we know it is an engine fault. Next is the "0", we know that it is a generic fault. Then we have a 3, by looking at the above paragraph, we will see that the "3" relates to the Ignition System/Misfire. Last, we have the "01". In this case, the last two numbers tell you which cylinder is misfiring. Put this together, and we have an engine fault, with cylinder number three misfiring. If it were P0300, then it is a multiple misfire; meaning there are too many cylinders misfiring, and the control unit can't determine which one it is.

Specific self-diagnostic on-board monitoring of emission malfunctions

Wow, that sounds complex. It really is not! Ford and GM call this the Diagnostic Executive. Daimler Chrysler calls it the Task Manager. This is OBDII compliant software, which is a program inside the PCM that observes all that is happening. The PCM is a workhorse. It performs immense calculations in microseconds. It has to control: when the injectors open and close, when to fire the coil, when to advance the timing on the cams, and in the ignition and so on. While all this is happening, the OBDII software is checking on all these components to see if they are operating properly. The software:

- Controls the status of the MIL
- Stores DTCs and the Freeze Frame dat
- Checks the drive cycles that control the DTCs
- Starts and runs the monitors for the components
- Prioritizes the monitors
- Updates the readiness status for all the monitors
- Displays the tests results for the monitors

OBD II DIAGNOSTIC

• Makes sure that the monitors don't conflict with each other

As seen above, in order for the software to complete its job, it must perform and complete monitors on the engine management system. What is a monitor? Simply put, a monitor is a test run by the OBDII software in the PCM to check on emission related components to see if they are running properly. According to OBDII, there are two types of monitors:

• Continuous Monitor - this monitor continuously runs once its conditions are met.
• Non-Continuous Monitor - this is a monitor that is run only once per trip.

For a complete list and explanation of all monitors that are being done, please refer to chapter OBDII Scan Tools.

Monitors are important to OBDII. Like heart monitors, OBDII monitors are designed to test specific components in order to catch a malfunction or deterioration of the component that is being monitored. When a test fails, a DTC is then put into the PCMs memory.

Standardized component

As in any trade, there are different names and slang for the same word. Take fault code for instance. Some call it a code, others call it a fault, and still others call it "that thang that's broke". A DTC is a fault, code, or that " thang that's broke".

Before OBDII, each manufacturer had their own name for each component. I failed the first SAE test I took, since I was familiar with the terms used with European vehicles. The SAE tests used terms used with American vehicles. Now, since OBDII, all vehicles must use the same name for each component, and life is much easier for repairing cars and ordering parts.

Emissions terminology

As always when a governmental organization is involved, acronyms, and jargon is a must. The SAE came up with a standardized list of terminology for the components that pertain to OBDII. The standard is J1930. The OBDII Diagnostic Secrets Revealed book contains a complete list of Acronyms and Term definitions.

SECRETS REVEALED

OBD II FAULT CODES

GENERIC

P0100	Mass or Volume Air Flow Circuit Malfunction
P0101	Mass or Volume Air Flow Circuit, Range/Performance
P0102	Mass or Volume Air Flow Circuit, Low Input
P0103	Mass or Volume Air Flow Circuit, High Input
P0104	Mass or Volume Air Flow Circuit Intermittent
P0105	Manifold Absolute Pressure/Barometric Pressure Circuit Malfunction
P0106	Manifold Absolute Pressure or Barometric Pressure, Range/Performance
P0107	Manifold Absolute Pressure or Barometric Pressure, Low Input
P0108	Manifold Absolute Pressure or Barometric Pressure, High Input
P0109	Manifold Absolute Pressure/Barometric Pressure Circuit Intermittent
P0110	Intake Air Temperature Circuit Malfunction
P0111	Intake Air Temperature Circuit Range/Performance
P0112	Intake Air Temperature Circuit, Low Input
P0113	Intake Air Temperature Circuit, High Input
P0114	Intake Air Temperature Circuit Intermittent
P0115	Engine Coolant Temperature Circuit Malfunction
P0116	Engine Coolant Temperature Circuit, Range/Performance
P0117	Engine Coolant Temperature Circuit, Low Input
P0118	Engine Coolant Temperature Circuit, High Input
P0119	Engine Coolant Temperature Circuit, Intermittent
P0120	Throttle/Pedal Position Sensor A Circuit, Malfunction
P0121	Throttle/Pedal Position Sensor A Circuit, Range/Performance
P0122	Throttle/Pedal Position Sensor A Circuit, Low Input
P0123	Throttle/Pedal Position Sensor A Circuit, High Input
P0124	Throttle Position Sensor A Circuit Intermittent

OBD II FAULT CODES

GENERIC

P0125	Insufficient Coolant Temperature for Closed, Loop Fuel Control
P0126	Insufficient Coolant Temperature for Stable Operation
P0128	Coolant Thermostat/Valve, Temperature below control range
P0130	O2 Sensor Circuit, Bank1-Sensor1, Malfunction
P0131	O2 Sensor Circuit, Bank1-Sensor1, Low Voltage
P0132	O2 Sensor Circuit, Bank1-Sensor1, High Voltage
P0133	O2 Sensor Circuit, Bank1-Sensor1, Slow Response
P0134	O2 Sensor Circuit, Bank1-Sensor1, No Activity Detected
P0135	O2 Sensor Heater Circuit, Bank1-Sensor1, Malfunction
P0136	O2 Sensor Circuit, Bank1-Sensor2, Malfunction
P0137	O2 Sensor Circuit, Bank1-Sensor2, Low Voltage
P0138	O2 Sensor Circuit, Bank1-Sensor2, High Voltage
P0139	O2 Sensor Circuit, Bank1-Sensor2, Slow Response
P0140	O2 Sensor Circuit, Bank1-Sensor2, No Activity Detected
P0141	O2 Sensor Heater Circuit, Bank1-Sensor2, Malfunction
P0142	O2 Sensor Circuit Malfunction (Bank 1, Sensor 3)
P0143	O2 Sensor Circuit Low Voltage (Bank 1, Sensor 3)
P0144	O2 Sensor Circuit High Voltage (Bank 1, Sensor 3)
P0145	O2 Sensor Circuit Slow Response (Bank 1, Sensor 3)
P0146	O2 Sensor Circuit No Activity Detected (Bank 1, Sensor 3)
P0147	O2 Sensor Heater Circuit Malfunction (Bank 1, Sensor 3)
P0150	O2 Sensor Circuit, Bank2-Sensor1, Malfunction
P0151	O2 Sensor Circuit, Bank2-Sensor1, Low Voltage
P0152	O2 Sensor Circuit, Bank2-Sensor1, High Voltage
P0153	O2 Sensor Circuit, Bank2-Sensor1, Slow Response

GENERIC

P0154	O2 Sensor Circuit, Bank2-Sensor1, No Activity Detected
P0155	O2 Sensor Heater Circuit, Bank2-Sensor1, Malfunction
P0156	O2 Sensor Circuit, Bank2-Sensor2, Malfunction
P0157	O2 Sensor Circuit, Bank2-Sensor2, Low Voltage
P0158	O2 Sensor Circuit, Bank2-Sensor2, High Voltage
P0159	O2 Sensor Circuit, Bank2-Sensor2, Slow Response
P0160	O2 Sensor Circuit, Bank2-Sensor2, No Activity Detected
P0161	O2 Sensor Heater Circuit, Bank2-Sensor2, Malfunction
P0162	O2 Sensor Circuit Malfunction (Bank 2, Sensor 3)
P0163	O2 Sensor Circuit Low Voltage (Bank 2, Sensor 3)
P0164	O2 Sensor Circuit High Voltage (Bank 2, Sensor 3)
P0165	O2 Sensor Circuit Slow Response (Bank 2, Sensor 3)
P0166	O2 Sensor Circuit No Activity Detected (Bank 2, Sensor 3)
P0167	O2 Sensor Heater Circuit Malfunction (Bank 2, Sensor 3)
P0170	Fuel Trim, Bank1, Malfunction
P0171	Fuel Trim, Bank1, System too Lean
P0172	Fuel Trim, Bank1, System too Rich
P0173	Fuel Trim, Bank2, Malfunction
P0174	Fuel Trim, Bank2, System too Lean
P0175	Fuel Trim, Bank2, System too Rich
P0176	Fuel Composition Sensor Circuit Malfunction
P0177	Fuel Composition Sensor Circuit Range/performance
P0178	Fuel Composition Sensor Circuit Low Input
P0179	Fuel Composition Sensor Circuit High Input
P0180	Fuel Temperature Sensor A Circuit Malfunction

GENERIC

P0181	Fuel Temperature Sensor A Circuit Range/Performance
P0182	Fuel Temperature Sensor A Circuit Low Input
P0183	Fuel Temperature Sensor A Circuit High Input
P0184	Fuel Temperature Sensor A Circuit Intermittent
P0185	Fuel Temperature Sensor B Circuit Malfunction
P0186	Fuel Temperature Sensor B Circuit Range/Performance
P0187	Fuel Temperature Sensor B Circuit Low Input
P0188	Fuel Temperature Sensor B Circuit High Input
P0189	Fuel Temperature Sensor B Circuit Intermittent
P0190	Fuel Rail Pressure Sensor Circuit Malfunction
P0191	Fuel Rail Pressure Sensor Circuit Range/Performance
P0192	Fuel Rail Pressure Sensor Circuit Low Input
P0193	Fuel Rail Pressure Sensor Circuit High Input
P0194	Fuel Rail Pressure Sensor Intermittent
P0195	Engine Oil Temperature Sensor Malfunction
P0196	Engine Oil Temperature Sensor Range/Performance
P0197	Engine Oil Temperature Sensor Low
P0198	Engine Oil Temperature Sensor High
P0199	Engine Oil Temperature Sensor Intermittent
P0200	Injector Circuit Malfunction
P0201	Injector Circuit Malfunction - Cylinder 1
P0202	Injector Circuit Malfunction - Cylinder 2
P0203	Injector Circuit Malfunction - Cylinder 3
P0204	Injector Circuit Malfunction - Cylinder 4
P0205	Injector Circuit Malfunction - Cylinder 5

GENERIC

P0206	Injector Circuit Malfunction - Cylinder 6
P0207	Injector Circuit Malfunction - Cylinder 7
P0208	Injector Circuit Malfunction - Cylinder 8
P0209	Injector Circuit Malfunction - Cylinder 9
P0210	Injector Circuit Malfunction - Cylinder 10
P0211	Injector Circuit Malfunction - Cylinder 11
P0212	Injector Circuit Malfunction - Cylinder 12
P0213	Cold Start Injector 1 Malfunction
P0214	Cold Start Injector 2 Malfunction
P0215	Engine Shutoff Solenoid Malfunction
P0216	Injection Timing Control Circuit Malfunction
P0217	Engine Over Temperature Condition
P0218	Transmission Over Temperature Condition
P0219	Engine Over Speed Condition
P0220	Throttle/Pedal Position Sensor/Switch B Circuit Malfunction
P0221	Throttle/Pedal Position Sensor/Switch B Circuit Range/Performance
P0222	Throttle/Pedal Position Sensor/Switch B Circuit Low Input
P0223	Throttle/Pedal Position Sensor/Switch B Circuit High Input
P0224	Throttle/Pedal Position Sensor/Switch B Circuit Intermittent
P0225	Throttle/Pedal Position Sensor/Switch C Circuit Malfunction
P0226	Throttle/Pedal Position Sensor/Switch C Circuit Range/Performance
P0227	Throttle/Pedal Position Sensor/Switch C Circuit Low Input
P0228	Throttle/Pedal Position Sensor/Switch C Circuit High Input
P0229	Throttle/Pedal Position Sensor/Switch C Circuit Intermittent
P0230	Fuel Pump Primary Circuit Malfunction

OBD II FAULT CODES

GENERIC

P0231	Fuel Pump Secondary Circuit Low
P0232	Fuel Pump Secondary Circuit High
P0233	Fuel Pump Secondary Circuit Intermittent
P0234	Turbocharger Overboost Condition, Control limit exceeded
P0235	Turbocharger Boost Sensor (A) Circuit Malfunction
P0236	Turbocharger Boost Sensor (A) Circuit, Range/Performance
P0237	Turbocharger Boost Sensor (A) Circuit, Low Input.
P0238	Turbocharger Boost Sensor (A) Circuit, High Input
P0239	Turbocharger Boost Sensor (B) Circuit Malfunction
P0240	Turbocharger Boost Sensor (B) Circuit Range/Performance
P0241	Turbocharger Boost Sensor (B) Circuit low
P0242	Turbocharger Boost Sensor (B) Circuit high
P0243	Turbocharger Wastegate Solenoid A Malfunction
P0244	Turbocharger Wastegate Solenoid A Range/Performance
P0245	Turbocharger Wastegate Solenoid A Low
P0246	Turbocharger Wastegate Solenoid A High
P0247	Turbocharger Wastegate Solenoid B Malfunction
P0248	Turbocharger Wastegate Solenoid B Range/Performance
P0249	Turbocharger Wastegate Solenoid B Low
P0250	Turbocharger Wastegate Solenoid B High
P0251	Injection Pump A Rotor/Cam Malfunction
P0252	Injection Pump A Rotor/Cam Range/Performance
P0253	Injection Pump A Rotor/Cam Low
P0254	Injection Pump A Rotor/Cam High
P0255	Injection Pump A Rotor/Cam Intermittent

GENERIC

P0256	Injection Pump B Rotor/Cam Malfunction
P0257	Injection Pump B Rotor/Cam Range/Performance
P0258	Injection Pump B Rotor/Cam Low
P0259	Injection Pump B Rotor/Cam High
P0260	Injection Pump B Rotor/Cam Intermittent
P0261	Cylinder 1 Injector Circuit Low
P0262	Cylinder 1 Injector Circuit High
P0263	Cylinder 1 Injector Contribution/Balance Fault
P0264	Cylinder 2 Injector Circuit Low
P0265	Cylinder 2 Injector Circuit High
P0266	Cylinder 2 Injector Contribution/Balance Fault
P0267	Cylinder 3 Injector Circuit Low
P0268	Cylinder 3 Injector Circuit High
P0269	Cylinder 3 Injector Contribution/Balance Fault
P0270	Cylinder 4 Injector Circuit Low
P0271	Cylinder 4 Injector Circuit High
P0272	Cylinder 4 Injector Contribution/Balance Fault
P0273	Cylinder 5 Injector Circuit Low
P0274	Cylinder 5 Injector Circuit High
P0275	Cylinder 5 Injector Contribution/Balance Fault
P0276	Cylinder 6 Injector Circuit Low
P0277	Cylinder 6 Injector Circuit High
P0278	Cylinder 6 Injector Contribution/Balance Fault
P0279	Cylinder 7 Injector Circuit Low
P0280	Cylinder 7 Injector Circuit High

OBD II FAULT CODES

GENERIC

P0281	Cylinder 7 Injector Contribution/Balance Fault
P0282	Cylinder 8 Injector Circuit Low
P0283	Cylinder 8 Injector Circuit High
P0284	Cylinder 8 Injector Contribution/Balance Fault
P0285	Cylinder 9 Injector Circuit Low
P0286	Cylinder 9 Injector Circuit High
P0287	Cylinder 9 Injector Contribution/Balance Fault
P0288	Cylinder 10 Injector Circuit Low
P0289	Cylinder 10 Injector Circuit High
P0290	Cylinder 10 Injector Contribution/Balance Fault
P0291	Cylinder 11 Injector Circuit Low
P0292	Cylinder 11 Injector Circuit High
P0293	Cylinder 11 Injector Contribution/Balance Fault
P0294	Cylinder 12 Injector Circuit Low
P0295	Cylinder 12 Injector Circuit High
P0296	Cylinder 12 Injector Contribution/Balance Fault
P0300	Random/Multiple Cylinder, Misfire Detected
P0301	Cylinder 1, Misfire Detected
P0302	Cylinder 2, Misfire Detected
P0303	Cylinder 3, Misfire Detected
P0304	Cylinder 4, Misfire Detected
P0305	Cylinder 5, Misfire Detected
P0306	Cylinder 6, Misfire Detected
P0307	Cylinder 7, Misfire Detected
P0308	Cylinder 8, Misfire Detected

GENERIC

P0309	Cylinder 9 Misfire Detected
P0310	Cylinder 10 Misfire Detected
P0311	Cylinder 11 Misfire Detected
P0312	Cylinder 12 Misfire Detected
P0313	Misfire Detected, Low Fuel Level
P0314	Single Cylinder Misfire
P0320	Ignition/Distributor Engine Speed Input Cir. Malfunction
P0321	Ignition/Distributor Eng.Speed Inp.Circ, Range/Performance
P0322	Ignition/Distributor Eng.Speed Inp.Circ, No Signal
P0323	Ignition/Distributor Eng.Speed Inp.Circ, Intermittent
P0325	Knock Sensor 1 Circuit Malfunction (Bank 1)
P0326	Knock Sensor 1 Circuit Range/Performance (Bank 1)
P0327	Knock Sensor 1 Circuit, Low Input
P0328	Knock Sensor 1 Circuit, High Input
P0329	Knock Sensor 1 Circuit Intermittent (Bank 1)
P0330	Knock Sensor 2 Circuit Malfunction (Bank 2)
P0331	Knock Sensor 2 Circuit Range/Performance (Bank 2)
P0332	Knock Sensor 2 Circuit, Low Input
P0333	Knock Sensor 2 Circuit, High Input
P0334	Knock Sensor 2 Circuit Intermittent (Bank 2)
P0335	Crankshaft Position Sensor A Circuit Malfunction
P0336	Crankshaft Position Sensor A Circuit Range/Performance
P0337	Crankshaft Position Sensor (A) Circuit, Low Input
P0338	Crankshaft Position Sensor A Circuit High Input
P0339	Crankshaft Position Sensor A Circuit Intermittent

GENERIC

P0340	Camshaft Position Sensor Circuit Malfunction
P0341	Camshaft Position Sensor Circuit, Range/Performance
P0342	Camshaft Position Sensor Circuit, Low Input
P0343	Camshaft Position Sensor Circuit, High Input
P0344	Camshaft Position Sensor Circuit Intermittent
P0350	Ignition Coil Primary/Secondary Circuit Malfunction
P0351	Ignition Coil A Primary/Secondary Circuit Malfunction
P0352	Ignition Coil B Primary/Secondary Circuit Malfunction
P0353	Ignition Coil C Primary/Secondary Circuit Malfunction
P0354	Ignition Coil D Primary/Secondary Circuit Malfunction
P0355	Ignition Coil E Primary/Secondary Circuit Malfunction
P0356	Ignition Coil F Primary/Secondary Circuit Malfunction
P0357	Ignition Coil G Primary/Secondary Circuit Malfunction
P0358	Ignition Coil H Primary/Secondary Circuit Malfunction
P0359	Ignition Coil I Primary/Secondary Circuit Malfunction
P0360	Ignition Coil J Primary/Secondary Circuit Malfunction
P0361	Ignition Coil K Primary/Secondary Circuit Malfunction
P0362	Ignition Coil L Primary/Secondary Circuit Malfunction
P0370	Timing Ref High Resolution Signal A Malfunction
P0371	Timing Ref High Resolution Signal A Too Many Pulses
P0372	Timing Ref High Resolution Signal A Too Few Pulses
P0373	Timing Ref High Resolution Signal A Erratic Pulses
P0374	Timing Ref High Resolution Signal A No Pulses
P0375	Timing Ref High Resolution Signal B Malfunction
P0376	Timing Ref High Resolution Signal B Too Many Pulses

GENERIC

P0377	Timing Ref High Resolution Signal B Too Few Pulses
P0378	Timing Ref High Resolution Signal B Erratic Pulses
P0379	Timing Ref High Resolution Signal B No Pulses
P0380	Glow Plug/Heater Circuit Malfunction
P0381	Glow Plug/Heater Indicator Circuit Malfunction
P0385	Crankshaft Position Sensor B Circuit Malfunction
P0386	Crankshaft Position Sensor B Circuit Range/Performance
P0387	Crankshaft Position Sensor B Circuit Low Input
P0388	Crankshaft Position Sensor B Circuit High Input
P0389	Crankshaft Position Sensor B Circuit Intermittent
P0400	Exhaust Gas Recirculation Flow, Malfunction
P0401	Exhaust Gas Recirculation Flow, Insufficient Detected
P0402	Exhaust Gas Recirculation Flow, Excessive Detected
P0403	Exhaust Gas Recirculation Circuit Malfunction
P0404	Exhaust Gas Recirculation Circuit Range/Performance
P0405	Exhaust Gas Recirculation Sensor A Circuit Low
P0406	Exhaust Gas Recirculation Sensor A Circuit High
P0407	Exhaust Gas Recirculation Sensor B Circuit Low
P0408	Exhaust Gas Recirculation Sensor B Circuit High
P0410	Secondary Air Injection System, Malfunction
P0411	Secondary Air Injection System, Incorrect Flow Detected
P0412	Secondary Air Injection System Switching Valve A Circuit, Malfunction
P0413	Secondary Air Injection System Switching Valve A Circuit Open
P0414	Secondary Air Injection System Switching Valve A Circuit Shorted
P0415	Secondary Air Injection System Switching Valve B Circuit Malfunction

OBD II FAULT CODES

GENERIC

P0416	Secondary Air Injection System Switching Valve B Circuit Open
P0417	Secondary Air Injection System Switching Valve B Circuit Shorted
P0418	Secondary Air Injection System Relay A circuit malfunction
P0419	Secondary Air Injection System Relay B circuit malfunction
P0420	Catalyst System, Bank1, Efficiency Below Threshold
P0422	Main Catalyst, Bank1, Efficiency Below Threshold
P0423	Heated Catalyst Efficiency Below Threshold (Bank 1)
P0424	Heated Catalyst Temperature Below Threshold (Bank 1)
P0430	Catalyst Sys Efficiency Below Threshold (Bank 2)
P0431	Warm Up Catalyst Efficiency Below Threshold (Bank 2)
P0432	Main Catalyst, Bank2, Efficiency Below Threshold
P0433	Heated Catalyst Efficiency Below Threshold (Bank 2)
P0434	Heated Catalyst Temperature Below Threshold (Bank 2)
P0440	Evaporative Emission Control System, Malfunction
P0441	Evaporative Emission Control System Incorrect, Purge Flow
P0442	Evaporative Emission Control System (small leak), Leak Detected
P0443	Evaporative Emission Control System Purge Control Valve Circuit Malfunction
P0444	Evaporative Emission Control System Purge Control Valve Circuit Open
P0445	Evaporative Emission Control System Purge Control Valve Circuit Shorted
P0446	Evaporative Emission Control System Pressure Sensor Malfunction
P0446	Evaporative Emission Control System vent control circuit Malfunction
P0447	Evaporative Emission Control System Pressure Sensor Malfunction
P0447	Evaporative Emission Control System vent control circuit open
P0448	Evaporative Emission Control System Pressure Sensor Malfunction
P0448	Evaporative Emission Control System vent control circuit shorted

GENERIC

P0449	Evaporative Emission Control System vent Valve/Sol circuit Malfunction
P0450	Evaporative Emission Control System Pressure Sensor Malfunction
P0451	Evaporative Emission Control System Pressure Sensor Range/Performance
P0452	Evaporative Emission Control System Pressure Sensor, Low Input
P0453	Evaporative Emission Control System Pressure Sensor, High Input
P0454	Evaporative Emission Control System Pressure Sensor Intermittent
P0455	Evaporative Emission Control System (gross leak), Leak Detected
P0460	Fuel Level Sensor Circuit Malfunction
P0461	Fuel Level Sensor Circuit, Range/Performance
P0462	Fuel Level Sensor Circuit Low Input
P0463	Fuel Level Sensor Circuit High Input
P0464	Fuel Level Sensor Circuit Intermittent
P0465	Purge Flow Sensor Circuit Malfunction
P0466	Purge Flow Sensor Circuit Range/Performance
P0467	Purge Flow Sensor Circuit Low Input
P0468	Purge Flow Sensor Circuit High Input
P0469	Purge Flow Sensor Circuit Intermittent
P0470	Exhaust Pressure Sensor Malfunction
P0471	Exhaust Pressure Sensor Range/Performance
P0472	Exhaust Pressure Sensor Low
P0473	Exhaust Pressure Sensor High
P0474	Exhaust Pressure Sensor Intermittent
P0475	Exhaust Pressure Control Valve Malfunction
P0476	Exhaust Pressure Control Valve Range/Performance
P0477	Exhaust Pressure Control Valve Low

GENERIC

P0478	Exhaust Pressure Control Valve High
P0479	Exhaust Pressure Control Valve Intermittent
P0500	Vehicle Speed Sensor Malfunction
P0501	Vehicle Speed Sensor, Range/Performance
P0502	Vehicle Speed Sensor Circuit Low Input
P0503	Vehicle Speed Sensor Erratic
P0505	Idle control system malfunction
P0506	Idle Control System, RPM Lower than Expected
P0507	Idle Control System, RPM Higher than Expected
P0510	Closed Throttle Position Switch, Malfunction
P0530	A/C Refrigerant Pressure Sensor Circuit Malfunction
P0531	A/C Refrigerant Pressure Sensor Circuit Range/Performance
P0532	A/C Refrigerant Pressure Sensor Circuit Low Input
P0533	A/C Refrigerant Pressure Sensor Circuit High Input
P0534	Air Conditioner Refrigerant Charge Low
P0550	Power Steering Pressure Sensor Circuit Malfunction
P0551	Power Steering Pressure Sensor Circuit Range/Performance
P0552	Power Steering Pressure Sensor Circuit Low Input
P0553	Power Steering Pressure Sensor Circuit High Input
P0554	Power Steering Pressure Sensor Circuit Intermittent
P0560	System Voltage, Malfunction
P0561	System Voltage Range/Performance
P0562	System Voltage, Low Voltage
P0563	System Voltage, High Voltage
P0565	Cruise Control On Signal Malfunction

GENERIC

P0566	Cruise Control Off Signal Malfunction
P0567	Cruise Control Resume Signal Malfunction
P0568	Cruise Control Set Signal Malfunction
P0569	Cruise Control Coast Signal Malfunction
P0570	Cruise Control Accel Signal Malfunction
P0571	Cruise/Brake Switch (A) Circuit, Malfunction
P0572	Cruise Control/Brake Switch A Circuit Low
P0573	Cruise Control/Brake Switch A Circuit High
P0600	Serial Link Malfunction
P0601	Internal Control Module Memory, Check Sum Error
P0602	Control Module Programming Error
P0603	Internal Control Module (KAM), Error
P0604	Internal Control Module Random Access, Memory (RAM) Error
P0605	Internal Control Module, ROM Test Error
P0606	PCM Processor Fault
P0700	Transmission Control System, Malfunction
P0701	Transmission Control System Range/Performance
P0702	Transmission Control System, Electrical
P0703	Torque Converter/Brake Switch B Circuit, Malfunction
P0704	Clutch Switch Input Circuit Malfunction
P0705	Transmission Range Sensor Circuit (PRNDL Inp.), Malfunction
P0706	Transmission Range Sensor Circuit, Range/Performance
P0707	Transmission Range Sensor Circuit, Low Input
P0708	Transmission Range Sensor Circuit High Input
P0709	Transmission Range Sensor Circuit Intermittent

OBD II FAULT CODES

GENERIC

P0710	Transmission Fluid Temperature Sensor Circuit, Malfunction
P0711	Transmission Fluid Temperature Sensor Circuit, Range/Performance
P0712	Transmission Fluid Temperature Sensor Circuit, Low Input
P0713	Transmission Fluid Temperature Sensor Circuit, High Input
P0714	Transmission Fluid Temperature Sensor Circuit Intermittent
P0715	Input Turbine/Speed Sensor Circuit, Malfunction
P0716	Input Turbine/Speed Sensor Circuit, Range/Performance
P0717	Input/Turbine Speed Sensor Circuit, No Signal
P0718	Input/Turbine Speed Sensor Circuit Intermittent
P0719	Torque Converter/Brake Switch B Circuit Low
P0720	Output Speed Sensor Circuit Malfunction
P0721	Output Speed Sensor Circuit, Range/Performance
P0722	Output Speed Sensor Circuit, No Signal
P0723	Output Speed Sensor Circuit Intermittent
P0724	Torque Converter/Brake Switch B Circuit High
P0725	Engine Speed Inp. Circuit, Malfunction
P0726	Engine Speed Inp. Circuit, Range/Performance
P0727	Engine Speed Inp. Circuit, No Signal
P0728	Engine Speed Input Circuit Intermittent
P0730	Gear, Incorrect Ratio
P0731	Gear 1 Incorrect Ratio
P0732	Gear, 2 Incorrect Ratio
P0733	Gear, 3 Incorrect Ratio
P0734	Gear, 4 Incorrect Ratio
P0735	Gear, 5 Incorrect Ratio

GENERIC

P0736	Reverse Incorrect Ratio
P0740	Torque Converter Clutch Circuit, Malfunction
P0741	Torque Converter Clutch Circuit, Performance or Stuck Off
P0742	Torque Converter Clutch Circuit Stuck On
P0743	Torque Converter Clutch Circuit Electrical
P0744	Torque Converter Clutch Circuit Intermittent
P0745	Pressure Control Solenoid Malfunction
P0746	Pressure Control Solenoid Performance or Stuck Off
P0747	Pressure Control Solenoid Stuck On
P0748	Pressure Control Solenoid, Electrical
P0749	Pressure Control Solenoid Intermittent
P0750	Shift Solenoid A Malfunction
P0751	Shift Solenoid A, Performance or Stuck Off
P0752	Shift Solenoid A, Stuck On
P0753	Shift Solenoid A, Electrical
P0754	Shift Solenoid A Intermittent
P0755	Shift Solenoid B Malfunction
P0756	Shift Solenoid B, Performance or Stuck Off
P0757	Shift Solenoid B, Stuck On
P0758	Shift Solenoid B, Electrical
P0759	Shift Solenoid B Intermittent
P0760	Shift Solenoid C Malfunction
P0761	Shift Solenoid C, Performance or Stuck Off
P0762	Shift Solenoid C, Stuck On
P0763	Shift Solenoid C, Electrical

GENERIC

P0764	Shift Solenoid C Intermittent
P0765	Shift Solenoid D Malfunction
P0766	Shift Solenoid D Performance or Stuck Off
P0767	Shift Solenoid D Stuck On
P0768	Shift Solenoid D, Electrical
P0769	Shift Solenoid D Intermittent
P0770	Shift Solenoid E Malfunction
P0771	Shift Solenoid E Performance or Stuck Off
P0772	Shift Solenoid E Stuck On
P0773	Shift Solenoid E, Electrical
P0774	Shift Solenoid E Intermittent
P0780	Shift Malfunction
P0781	1-2 Shift Malfunction
P0782	2-3 Shift Malfunction
P0783	3-4 Shift Malfunction
P0784	4-5 Shift Malfunction
P0785	Shift/Timing Solenoid Malfunction
P0786	Shift/Timing Solenoid Range/Performance
P0787	Shift/Timing Solenoid Low
P0788	Shift/Timing Solenoid High
P0789	Shift/Timing Solenoid Intermittent
P0790	Normal/Performance Switch Circuit, Malfunction
P0801	Reverse Inhibit Control Circuit Malfunction
P0803	1-4 Upshift (Skip Shift) Solenoid Control Circuit Malfunction
P0804	1-4 Upshift (Skip Shift) Lamp Control Circuit Malfunction

GENERIC

P0805	Supercharger function
P0806	Magnetic supercharger clutch (Y2/1)
P0809	Angle deviation between camshaft and crankshaft
P0811	CAN from electronic lock

OBD II FAULT CODES

BMW

P1083	Fuel control limit mixture too lean (bank 1 sensor 1)
P1084	Fuel control limit mixture too rich (bank 1 sensor 1)
P1085	Fuel control limit mixture too lean (bank 2 sensor 1)
P1086	Fuel control limit mixture too rich (bank 2 sensor 1)
P1087	O2 sensor circuit slow response in lean control range (bank 1 sensor 1)
P1088	O2 sensor circuit slow response in rich control range (bank 1 sensor 1)
P1089	O2 sensor circuit slow response in lean control range (bank 1 sensor 2)
P1090	Pre catalyst fuel trim system too lean bank 1
P1091	Pre catalyst fuel trim system too rich bank 1
P1092	Pre catalyst fuel trim system too lean bank 2
P1093	Pre catalyst fuel trim system too rich bank 2
P1094	O2 sensor circuit slow response in rich control range (bank 2 sensor 1)
P1095	O2 sensor signal circuit slow switching from lean to rich (bank 1 sensor 1)
P1096	O2 sensor signal circuit slow switching from lean to rich (bank 2 sensor 1)
P1097	O2 sensor circuit slow response after coast down fuel cut-off (bank 1 sensor 2)
P1098	O2 sensor circuit slow response after coast down fuel cut-off (bank 2 sensor 2)
P1111	Engine coolant temperature radiator outlet sensor low input
P1112	Engine coolant temperature radiator outlet sensor high input
P1115	Coolant temperature sensor plausibility
P1116	Mass or volume air flow circuit range/performance problem (bank 2)
P1117	Mass or volume air flow circuit low input (bank 2)
P1118	Mass or volume air flow circuit high input (bank 2)
P1120	Pedal position sensor circuit
P1121	Pedal position sensor 1 range/performance problem
P1122	Pedal position sensor 1 low input

BMW

P1123	Pedal position sensor 1 high input
P1132	O2 sensor heater control circuit (bank 1 sensor 1)
P1133	O2 sensor heater control circuit (bank 2 sensor 1)
P1134	O2 sensor heater circuit signal intermittent (bank 1 sensor 1)
P1135	O2 sensor heater circuit low voltage (bank 1 sensor 1)
P1136	O2 sensor heater circuit high voltage (bank 1 sensor 1)
P1137	O2 sensor heater circuit signal intermittent (bank 1 sensor 2)
P1138	O2 Sensor heater circuit low voltage (bank 1 sensor 2)
P1139	O2 sensor heater circuit high voltage (bank 1 sensor 2)
P1140	Mass or volume air flow circuit range/performance problem
P1145	Solenoid valve running losses control circuit electrical
P1151	O2 sensor heater circuit signal intermittent (bank 2 sensor 1)
P1152	O2 sensor heater circuit low voltage (bank 2 sensor 1)
P1153	O2 sensor heater circuit high voltage (bank 2 sensor 1)
P1155	O2 sensor heater circuit signal intermittent (bank 2 sensor 2)
P1156	O2 sensor heater circuit low voltage (bank 2 sensor 2)
P1157	O2 sensor heater circuit high voltage (bank 2 sensor 2)
P1158	Fuel trim adaptation additive bank 1 low
P1159	Fuel trim adaptation additive bank 1 high
P1160	Fuel trim adaptation additive bank 2 low
P1161	Fuel trim adaptation additive bank 2 high M52: Engine oil temperature sensor circuit
P1162	Fuel trim adaptation additive per ignition bank 1 low
P1163	Fuel trim adaptation additive per ignition bank 1 high
P1164	Fuel trim adaptation additive per ignition bank 2 low
P1165	Fuel trim adaptation additive per ignition bank 2 high

BMW

P1174	Fuel trim adaptation additive bank 1 malfunction
P1175	Fuel trim adaptation additive bank 2 malfunction
P1176	O2 sensor slow response bank 1
P1177	O2 sensor slow response bank 2
P1178	O2 sensor signal circuit slow switching from rich to lean (bank 1 sensor 1)
P1179	O2 sensor signal circuit slow switching from rich to lean (bank 2 sensor 1)
P1180	O2 sensor signal circuit slow switching from rich to lean (bank 1 sensor 2)
P1181	O2 sensor signal circuit slow switching from rich to lean (bank 2 sensor 2)
P1182	O2 sensor (bank 1 sensor 2) open circuit during coast down fuel cut-off
P1183	O2 sensor (bank 2 sensor 2) open circuit during coast down fuel cut-off
P1186	O2 sensor heater control circuit (bank 1 sensor 2)
P1187	O2 sensor heater control circuit (bank 2 sensor 2)
P1188	Fuel control (bank 1 sensor 1)
P1189	Fuel control (bank 2 sensor 1)
P1190	Pre catalyst fuel trim system bank 1
P1191	Pre catalyst fuel trim system bank 2
P1192	Post catalyst fuel trim system bank 1
P1193	Post catalyst fuel trim system bank 2
P1221	Pedal position sensor 2 range/performance problem
P1222	Pedal position sensor 2 low input
P1223	Pedal position sensor 2 high input
P1270	Control module self-test, torque monitoring M73: Mass air flow sensor bank comparison plausibility
P1271	Ambient air pressure sensor electrical
P1283	Switching solenoid for air assisted injection valves bank 1 control circuit electrical
P1284	Switching solenoid for air assisted injection valves bank 1 control circuit signal low

BMW

P1285	Switching solenoid for air assisted injection valves bank 1 control circuit signal high
P1287	Switching solenoid for air assisted injection valves bank 2 control circuit electrical
P1288	Switching solenoid for air assisted injection valves bank 2 control circuit signal low
P1289	Switching solenoid for air assisted injection valves bank 2 control circuit signal high
P1313	'A' Camshaft position actuator plausibility
P1317	'B' Camshaft position actuator plausibility
P1327	Knock sensor 2 (bank 1) low input
P1328	Knock sensor 2 (bank 1) high input
P1332	Knock sensor 4 low input
P1333	Knock sensor 4 high input
P1340	Multiple cylinder misfire during start
P1341	Multiple cylinder misfire with fuel cut-off
P1342	Misfire during start cylinder 1
P1343	Misfire cylinder 1 with fuel cut-off
P1344	Misfire during start cylinder 2
P1345	Misfire cylinder 2 with fuel cut-off
P1346	Misfire during start cylinder 3
P1347	Misfire cylinder 3 with fuel cut-off
P1348	Misfire during start cylinder 4
P1349	Misfire cylinder 4 fuel cut-off
P1350	Misfire during start cylinder 5
P1351	Misfire cylinder 5 with fuel cut-off
P1352	Misfire during start cylinder 6
P1353	Misfire cylinder 6 with fuel cut-off
P1354	Misfire during start cylinder 7

BMW

P1355	Misfire cylinder 7 with fuel cut-off
P1356	Misfire during start cylinder 8
P1357	Misfire cylinder 8 with fuel cut-off
P1358	Misfire during start cylinder 9
P1359	Misfire cylinder 9 with fuel cut-off
P1360	Misfire during start cylinder 10
P1361	Misfire cylinder 10 with fuel cut-off
P1362	Misfire during start cylinder 11
P1363	Misfire cylinder 11 with fuel cut-off
P1364	Misfire during start cylinder 12
P1365	Misfire cylinder 12 with fuel cut-off
P1384	Knock sensor 3 circuit
P1385	Knock sensor 4 circuit
P1386	Control module self-test, knock control circuit baseline test bank 1
P1396	Crankshaft position sensor segment timing plausibility
P1397	Camshaft position sensor 'B' circuit (bank1)
P1400	Heated catalyst battery voltage or current too low during heating (bank 1)
P1401	Heated catalyst current too high during heating (bank 1)
P1402	Heated catalyst power switch over temperature condition (bank 1)
P1403	Carbon canister shut-off valve control circuit electrical -or- M73: heated catalyst battery voltage or current too low during heating (bank 2)
P1404	Heated catalyst current too high during heating (bank 2)
P1405	Heated catalyst power switch over temperature condition (bank 2)
P1406	Heated catalyst internal control module checksum/ROM error
P1413	Secondary air injection pump relay control circuit signal low

BMW

P1414	Secondary air injection pump relay control circuit signal high
P1420	Secondary air valve control circuit electrical
P1421	Secondary air system bank 2
P1423	Secondary air system bank 1
P1432	Secondary air injection system incorrect flow detected
P1438	Purge control valve control open circuit
P1439	Purge control valve control circuit signal low
P1440	Purge control valve control circuit signal high
P1441	Leakage diagnostic pump control open circuit
P1442	Leakage diagnostic pump control circuit signal low
P1443	Leakage diagnostic pump control circuit signal high
P1444	Diagnostic module tank leakage (DM-TL) pump control open circuit
P1445	Diagnostic module tank leakage (DM-TL) pump control circuit signal low
P1446	Diagnostic module tank leakage (DM-TL) pump control circuit signal high
P1447	Diagnostic module tank leakage (DM-TL) pump current too high during switching solenoid test
P1448	Diagnostic module tank leakage (DM-TL) pump current too low during switching solenoid test
P1449	Diagnostic module tank leakage (DM-TL) pump current too high (during switching solenoid test)
P1450	Diagnostic module tank leakage (DM-TL) switching solenoid control open circuit
P1451	Diagnostic module tank leakage (DM-TL) switching solenoid control circuit signal low
P1452	Diagnostic module tank leakage (DM-TL) switching solenoid control circuit signal high
P1453	Secondary air injection pump relay control circuit electrical
P1454	Secondary air injection pump with series resistor control circuit electrical
P1456	Heated catalyst heater power supply open circuit (bank 1)
P1457	Heated catalyst power switch temperature sensor electrical (bank 1)
P1459	Heated catalyst heater power supply open circuit (bank 2)

BMW

P1460	Heated catalyst power switch temperature sensor electrical (bank 2)
P1461	Heated catalyst gate voltage signal low
P1462	Heated catalyst internal control module checksum/EEPROM error
P1463	Heated catalyst battery temperature sensor 1 electrical
P1464	Heated catalyst battery temperature sensor 2 electrical
P1465	Heated catalyst battery temperature sensor 1 or 2 plausibility
P1466	Heated catalyst power switch temperature sensor plausibility
P1467	Heated catalyst comparison battery voltages of power switches plausibility
P1468	Heated catalyst battery disconnecting switch plausibility
P1470	Leakage diagnostic pump control circuit electrical
P1472	Diagnostic module tank leakage (DM-TL) switching solenoid control circuit electrical
P1473	Diagnostic module tank leakage (DM-TL) pump current plausibility
P1475	Leakage diagnostic pump reed switch did not close
P1476	Leakage diagnostic pump clamped tube -or- M52 MY99/00: Leakage diagnostic pump reed switch circuit electrical
P1477	Leakage diagnostic pump reed switch did not open
P1500	Idle-speed control valve stuck open
P1501	Idle-speed control valve stuck closed
P1502	Idle-speed control valve closing solenoid control circuit signal high
P1503	Idle-speed control valve closing solenoid control circuit signal low
P1504	Idle-speed control valve closing solenoid control open circuit
P1505	Idle-speed control valve closing solenoid control circuit electrical
P1506	Idle-speed control valve opening solenoid control circuit signal high
P1507	Idle-speed control valve opening solenoid control circuit signal low
P1508	Idle-speed control valve opening solenoid control open circuit

BMW

P1509	Idle-speed control valve opening solenoid control circuit electrical
P1510	Idle-speed control valve stuck
P1511	DISA (differentiated intake manifold) control circuit electrical
P1512	DISA (differentiated intake manifold) control circuit signal low
P1513	DISA (differentiated intake manifold) control circuit signal high
P1519	'A' camshaft position actuator bank 1
P1520	'B' camshaft position actuator bank 1
P1522	'A' camshaft position actuator bank 2
P1523	'A' camshaft position actuator signal low bank 1 -or- M52: Camshaft position actuator tight or jammed
P1524	'A' camshaft position actuator control circuit signal high bank 1
P1525	'A' camshaft position actuator control open circuit bank 1
P1526	'A' camshaft position actuator control open circuit bank 2
P1527	'A' camshaft position actuator control circuit signal low bank 2
P1528	'A' camshaft position actuator control circuit signal high bank 2
P1529	'B' camshaft position actuator control circuit signal low bank 1
P1530	'B' camshaft position actuator control circuit signal high bank 1
P1531	'B' camshaft position actuator control open circuit bank 1
P1532	'B' camshaft position actuator control open circuit bank 2
P1533	'B' camshaft position actuator control circuit signal low bank 2
P1534	'B' camshaft position actuator control circuit signal high bank 2
P1540	Pedal position sensor
P1541	Pedal position sensor double error
P1542	Pedal position sensor electrical

BMW

P1543 ... P1546	Pedal position sensor
P1550	Idle-speed control valve closing solenoid control circuit electrical
P1552	"A" Camshaft position actuator control open circuit bank 1
P1556	'A' Camshaft position actuator control open circuit bank 1
P1560	'B' Camshaft position actuator control open circuit bank 1
P1564	Control module selection
P1565	'B' Camshaft position actuator control open circuit bank 1
P1569	'A' Camshaft position actuator control open circuit bank 2
P1573	Electronic control module sensor supply B low output -or- S54/S62: 'A' Camshaft position actuator control circuit signal low bank 2
P1580	Throttle valve mechanically stuck
P1581	'B' Camshaft position actuator control open circuit bank 2
P1589	Control module self-test, knock control test pulse bank 1
P1593	DISA (Differentiated intake manifold) control circuit electrical
P1594	'B' Camshaft position actuator control open circuit bank 2
P1602	Control module self-test, control module defective
P1603	Control module self-test, torque monitoring
P1604	Control module self-test, speed monitoring
P1607	CAN-Version
P1608	Serial communication link control module
P1609	Serial communication link EML (electronically engine-power regulation)
P1611	Serial communication link transmission control module
P1619	Map cooling thermostat control circuit signal low
P1620	Map cooling thermostat control circuit signal high

BMW

P1622	Map cooling thermostat control circuit electrical
P1623	Pedal position sensor potentiometer supply
P1624	Pedal position sensor potentiometer supply channel 1 electrical -or- M52: coolant thermostat (coolant temperature below thermostat regulating temperature)
P1625	Pedal position sensor potentiometer supply channel 2 electrical
P1632	Throttle valve adaptation; Adaptation conditions not met
P1633	Throttle valve adaptation; Limp-home position unknown
P1634	Throttle valve adaptation; Spring test failed
P1635	Throttle valve adaptation; Lower mechanical stop not adapted
P1636	Throttle valve control circuit
P1637	Throttle valve position control; Control deviation
P1638	Throttle valve position control; Throttle stuck temporarily
P1639	Throttle valve position control; Throttle stuck permanently
P1640	Internal control module (ROM/RAM) error
P1690	Malfunction indicator lamp (MIL) electrical
P1734	Pressure control solenoid 'B' electrical
P1738	Pressure control solenoid 'C' electrical
P1743	Pressure control solenoid 'E' electrical -or- M44/M52: Brake band electrical
P1744	Pressure control solenoid 'A' electrical
P1746	Transmission control module output stage
P1747	CAN-Bus monitoring
P1748	Transmission control module self-test
P1749	Secondary pressure solenoid communication error -or- M52: Transmission control module internal memory
P1750	Secondary pressure solenoid circuit range/performance -or- M44/M52/M62/M73: System voltage input low

BMW

P1751	Secondary pressure solenoid open circuit -or- M52: System voltage input high
P1761	Shift lock solenoid malfunction
P1765	CAN throttle valve
P1770	CAN torque interface
P1780	CAN torque reduction
P1E00	CAN bus
P1E05	Control panel cruise control
P1E30	Charge air pressure control
P3515	A/C capacity output

OBD II FAULT CODES

Chrysler / Dodge / Plymouth

P0031	Shorted low condition detected in the oxygen sensor 1/1 heater element control
P0032	Shorted high condition detected in the oxygen sensor 1/1 heater element control
P0037	Shorted low condition detected in the oxygen sensor 1/2 heater element control
P0038	Shorted high condition detected in the oxygen sensor 1/2 heater element control
P0043	Shorted low condition detected in the oxygen sensor 1/3 heater element control
P0044	Shorted high condition detected in the oxygen sensor 1/3 heater element control
P0051	Shorted low condition detected in the oxygen sensor 2/1 heater element control
P0052	Shorted high condition detected in the oxygen sensor 2/1 heater element control
P0057	Shorted low condition detected in the oxygen sensor 2/2 heater element control
P0058	Shorted high condition detected in the oxygen sensor 2/2 heater element control
P0071	Ambient air temperature sensor voltage irrational performance
P1105	Open or shorted condition detected in the baro read solenoid control circuit
P1192	Inlet air temperature sensor input below the minimum acceptable voltage (shorted)
P1193	Inlet air temperature sensor input above the maximum acceptable voltage (shorted)
P1194	Incorrect or irrational performance has been detected for the PWM
P1195	Slow switching oxygen sensor detected in bank 1/1 during catalyst monitor test
P1196	Slow switching oxygen sensor detected in bank 2/1 during catalyst monitor test
P1197	Slow switching oxygen sensor detected in bank 1/2 during catalyst monitor test
P1198	Radiator coolant temperature sensor input above the maximum acceptable voltage
P1199	Radiator coolant temperature sensor input below the minimum acceptable voltage
P1243	Open or shorted condition detected in the turbocharger surge valve solenoid control
P1280	Open or shorted condition detected in the fuel system relay control circuit
P1281	Engine coolant temperature remains below normal operating temperatures
P1282	Open or shorted condition detected in the fuel pump relay control circuit
P1288	Open or shorted condition detected in the short runner tuning valve (SRV) solenoid

Chrysler / Dodge / Plymouth

P1289	Open or shorted condition detected in the manifold tuning valve solenoid control
P1290	Compressed natural gas system pressure above normal operating range
P1291	Energizing heated air intake does not change intake air temperature sensor
P1292	Compressed natural gas pressure sensor reading above acceptable voltage
P1293	Compressed natural gas pressure sensor reading below acceptable voltage
P1294	Target RPM not achieved during drive idle condition (possible vacuum leak)
P1295	Loss of a 5 volt feed to the throttle position sensor has been detected
P1296	Loss of a 5 volt feed to the manifold pressure sensor has been detected
P1297	No difference is recognized between the MAP readings at engine idle
P1298	A prolonged lean condition is detected during Wide Open Throttle
P1299	Manifold pressure sensor signal does not correlate to throttle position sensor signal
P1388	Open or shorted condition detected in the automatic shutdown (ASD) relay control
P1389	No Z1 or Z2 voltage sensed when the auto shutdown relay is energized
P1390	Relationship between Cam and Crank signals not correct
P1391	Loss of the camshaft position sensor or crankshaft position sensor has occurred
P1398	PCM is unable to learn the crankshaft position sensor's signal
P1399	Open or shorted condition detected in the wait to start lamp circuit
P1403	Loss of 5 Volt feed to the EGR position sensor
P1476	Insufficient flow of secondary air injection detected during aspirator test
P1477	Excessive flow of secondary air injection detected during aspirator test
P1478	Internal ambient/battery temperature sensor input voltage out of an acceptable range
P1479	Open or shorted condition detected in the transmission fan relay circuit
P1480	Open or shorted condition detected in the positive crankcase ventilation (PCV)
P1481	EATX RPM pulse generator signal for misfire detection
P1482	Catalyst temperature sensor input below the minimum acceptable voltage (shorted)

Chrysler / Dodge / Plymouth

P1483	Catalyst temperature sensor input above the maximum acceptable voltage (shorted)
P1484	Catalyst overheat condition detected by the catalyst temperature sensor
P1485	Open or shorted condition detected in the air assist injection (AAI) solenoid circuit
P1486	Leak detection pump detected a pinched hose in the evaporative purge system
P1487	An open or shorted condition detected in the control circuit of the high speed radiator fan
P1488	Auxiliary 5 volt sensor feed is sensed to be below an acceptable limit
P1489	Open or shorted condition detected in the control circuit of the high speed radiator fan
P1490	Open or shorted condition detected in control circuit of the low speed radiator fan
P1491	Open or shorted condition detected in the radiator fan control relay control circuit
P1492	External ambient (battery) temperature sensor input above acceptable voltage
P1493	External ambient (battery) temperature sensor input below acceptable voltage
P1494	Incorrect input state detected for the leak detection pump (LDP) pressure switch
P1495	Open or shorted condition detected in the leak detection pump (LDP) solenoid circuit
P1496	5 Volt sensor feed is sensed to be below an acceptable limit
P1498	Open or shorted condition detected in the control circuit of the high speed radiator fan
P1499	Open or shorted condition detected in the hydraulic cooling fan solenoid control
P1594	Battery voltage sense input above target charging voltage during engine operation
P1595	Open or shorted condition detected in the speed control vacuum
P1596	Speed control muxed switch input above maximum acceptable voltage
P1597	Speed control muxed switch input below minimum acceptable voltage
P1598	A/C pressure sensor input above maximum acceptable voltage
P1599	A/C pressure sensor input below minimum acceptable voltage
P1602	Generic service PCM identifier indicating module has not been properly reprogrammmed
P1682	Battery voltage sense input below target charging voltage during engine operation
P1683	Open or shorted condition detected in the speed control servo power control circuit

Chrysler / Dodge / Plymouth

P1684	Battery has been disconnected within the last 50 starts (status indicator only)
P1685	Engine controller has received an invalid key from SKIM
P1686	No CCD/J1850 messages received from the Sentry Key Immobilizer Module (SKIM)
P1687	No CCD/J1850 messages received from the cluster control module
P1693	Fault generated in the companion engine control module
P1694	No CCD/J1850 messages received from the Engine Control Module (ECM)
P1695	No CCD/J1850 messages received from the Body Control Module (BCM)
P1696	Unsuccessful attempt to write to an EEPROM location by the control module
P1697	Unsuccessful attempt to update Service Reminder Indicator (SRI or EMR)
P1698	No CCD/J1850 messages received from the Transmission Control Module (TCM)
P1699	No CCD/J1850 messages received from the Climate Control Module (CCM)
P1719	Open or shorted condition detected in the transmission 2-3 gear lock-out solenoid
P1740	Rationality error detected in either the torque converter clutch (TCC) solenoid
P1756	Requested pressure and actual pressure are not within a tolerance band
P1757	Requested pressure and actual pressure are not within a tolerance band
P1762	Governor pressure sensor input greater than a calibration limit
P1763	Governor pressure sensor input above maximum acceptable voltage level
P1764	Governor pressure sensor input below minimum acceptable voltage level
P1765	Open or shorted condition is detected in the transmission relay control circuit
P1830	Open or shorted condition detected in the clutch pedal switch over-ride relay control
P1899	Incorrect input state detected for the park/neutral switch

OBD II FAULT CODES

FORD

B1355	Ignition Run Circuit Open or Short To Ground
B1359	Ignition Run/Acc Circuit Open Or Short To Ground
B1365	Ignition Start Circuit Short To Battery
P1000	OBD Systems Readiness Test Not Complete
P1001	KOER not able to complete, KOER aborted
P1100	Mass Air Flow Sensor Circuit Intermittent
P1101	Mass Air Flow Sensor Out Of Self Test Range
P1105	Dual Alternator Upper Fault
P1106	Dual Alternator Lower Fault
P1107	Dual Alternator Lower Circuit
P1108	Dual Alternator Battery Lamp Circuit
P1109	Intake Air Temperature B Circuit Intermittent
P1111	System Pass
P1112	Intake Air Temperature Circuit Intermittent
P1114	Intake Air Temperature B Circuit Low Input (Super/Turbo Charged engines)
P1115	Intake Air Temperature B Circuit High Input (Super/Turbo Charged engines)
P1116	Engine Coolant Temperature Sensor Out Of Self Test Range
P1117	Engine Coolant Temperature Sensor Circuit Intermittent
P1118	Manifold Air Temperature Circuit Low Input
P1119	Manifold Air Temperature Circuit High Input
P1120	Throttle Position Sensor A Out Of Range Low (Ratch too low)
P1121	Throttle Position Sensor A Inconsistent With Mass Air Flow Sensor
P1122	Pedal Position Sensor A Circuit Low Input
P1123	Pedal Position Sensor A Circuit High Input
P1124	Throttle Position Sensor A Out Of Self Test Range

FORD

P1125	Throttle Position Sensor A Intermittent
P1127	Exhaust Not Warm, Downstream O2 Sensor Not Tested
P1128	Upstream HO2S Sensors Swapped
P1129	Downstream HO2S Sensors Swapped
P1130	Lack Of HO2S11 Switches - Fuel Trim At Limit
P1131	Lack Of HO2S11 Switches - Sensor Indicates Lean
P1132	Lack Of HO2S11 Switches - Sensor Indicates Rich
P1133	Bank 1 Fuel Control Shifted Lean (FAOSC)
P1134	Bank 1 Fuel Control Shifted Rich (FAOSC)
P1135	Pedal Position Sensor A Circuit Intermittent
P1137	Lack Of HO2S12 Switches - Sensor Indicates Lean
P1138	Lack Of HO2S12 Switches - Sensor Indicates Rich
P1139	Water in Fuel Indicator Circuit
P1140	Water in Fuel Condition
P1141	Fuel Restriction Indicator Circuit
P1142	Fuel Restriction Condition
P1150	Lack Of HO2S21 Switches - Fuel Trim At Limit
P1151	Lack Of HO2S21 Switches - Sensor Indicates Lean
P1152	Lack Of HO2S21 Switches - Sensor Indicates Rich
P1153	Bank 2 Fuel Control Shifted Lean (FAOSC)
P1154	Bank 2 Fuel Control Shifted Rich (FAOSC)
P1155	Alternative Fuel Control Module Has Activated the MIL
P1157	Lack Of HO2S22 Switches - Sensor Indicates Lean
P1158	Lack Of HO2S22 Switches - Sensor Indicates Rich
P1168	Fuel Rail Pressure Sensor In Range But Low

FORD

P1169	Fuel Rail Pressure Sensor In Range But High
P1170	Engine Shut Off Solenoid
P1171	Rotor Sensor
P1172	Rotor Control
P1173	Rotor Calibration
P1174	Cam Sensor
P1175	Cam Control
P1176	Cam Calibration
P1177	Synchronization
P1178	Boltup Limits
P1180	Fuel Delivery System - Low
P1181	Fuel Delivery System - High
P1183	Engine Oil Temperature Sensor Circuit
P1184	Engine Oil Temperature Sensor Out Of Self Test Range
P1185	Fuel Pump Temperature Sensor High
P1186	Fuel Pump Temperature Sensor Low
P1187	Variant Selection
P1188	Calibration Memory
P1189	Pump Speed Signal
P1190	Calibration Resistor Out Of Range
P1191	Key Line Voltage
P1192	V External
P1193	EGR Driver Over Current
P1194	ECM/PCM A/D Converter
P1195	SCP HBCC Chip Failed to Initialize

FORD

P1196	Key Off Voltage High
P1197	Key Off Voltage Low
P1198	Pump Rotor Control Underfueling
P1209	Injector Control Pressure Peak Delta Test Fault
P1210	Injector Control Pressure Above Expected Level
P1211	Injector Control Pressure Above/Below Desired
P1212	Injector Control Pressure Not At Expected Level
P1214	Pedal Position Sensor B Circuit Intermittent
P1215	Pedal Position Sensor C Circuit Low Input
P1216	Pedal Position Sensor C Circuit High Input
P1217	Pedal Position Sensor C Circuit Intermittent
P1218	CID High
P1219	CID Low
P1220	Series Throttle Control System
P1221	Traction Control System
P1222	Traction Control Output Circuit
P1223	Pedal Position Sensor B Circuit High Input
P1224	Throttle Position Sensor B Out Of Self Test Range
P1227	Wastegate Failed Closed (Over pressure)
P1228	Wastegate Failed Open (Under pressure)
P1229	Charge Air Cooler Pump Driver
P1230	Fuel Pump Low Speed Malfunction (VLCM)
P1231	Fuel Pump Secondary Circuit Low, High Speed (VLCM)
P1232	Fuel Pump Speed Primary Circuit (Two speed fuel pump)
P1233	Fuel Pump Driver Module Disabled or Off Line (Fuel Pump Driver Module)

FORD

P1234	Fuel Pump Driver Module Disabled or Off Line (Fuel Pump Driver Module)
P1235	Fuel Pump Control out Of Range (Fuel Pump Driver Module/VLCM)
P1236	Fuel Pump Control Out Of Range (Fuel Pump Driver Module)
P1237	Fuel Pump Secondary Circuit (Fuel Pump Driver Module)
P1238	Fuel Pump Secondary Circuit (Fuel Pump Driver Module)
P1239	Speed Fuel Pump Positive Feed
P1243	Second Fuel Pump Fault or Ground Fault
P1244	Alternator Load High Input
P1245	Alternator Load Low Input
P1246	Alternator Load Input
P1247	Turbo Boost Pressure Low
P1248	Turbo Boost Pressure Not Detected
P1249	Wastegate Control Valve Performance
P1252	Pedal Correlation PDS1 and LPDS High
P1253	Pedal Correlation PDS1 and LPDS Low
P1254	Pedal Correlation PDS2 and LPDS High
P1255	Pedal Correlation PDS2 and LPDS Low
P1256	Pedal Correlation PDS1 and HPDS
P1257	Pedal Correlation PDS2 and HPDS
P1258	Pedal Correlation PDS1 and PDS2
P1260	Theft Detected, Vehicle Immobilized
P1261	Cylinder #1 High To Low Side Short
P1262	Cylinder #2 High To Low Side Short
P1263	Cylinder #3 High To Low Side Short
P1264	Cylinder #4 High To Low Side Short

FORD

P1265	Cylinder #5 High To Low Side Short
P1266	Cylinder #6 High To Low Side Short
P1267	Cylinder #7 High To Low Side Short
P1268	Cylinder #8 High To Low Side Short
P1270	Engine RPM or Vehicle Speed Limiter Reached
P1271	Cylinder #1 High To Low Side Open
P1272	Cylinder #2 High To Low Side Open
P1273	Cylinder #3 High To Low Side Open
P1274	Cylinder #4 High To Low Side Open
P1275	Cylinder #5 High To Low Side Open
P1276	Cylinder #6 High To Low Side Open
P1277	Cylinder #7 High To Low Side Open
P1278	Cylinder #8 High To Low Side Open
P1280	Injector Control Pressure Out of Range Low
P1281	Injector Control Pressure Out of Range High
P1282	Excessive Injector Control Pressure
P1283	Injector Pressure Regulator Circuit
P1284	Aborted KOER - Injector Control Pressure Failure
P1285	Cylinder Head Overtemperature Condition
P1286	Fuel Pulsewidth In Range But Lower Than Expected
P1287	Fuel Pulsewidth In Range But Higher Than Expected
P1288	Cylinder Head Temperature Sensor Out Of Self Test Range
P1289	Cylinder Head Temperature Sensor Circuit High Input
P1290	Cylinder Head Temperature Sensor Circuit Low Input
P1291	Injector High Side Short To GND Or VBATT - Bank 1

FORD

P1292	Injector High Side Short To GND Or VBATT - Bank 2
P1293	Injector High Side Open - Bank 1
P1294	Injector High Side Open - Bank 2
P1295	Injector Multiple Faults - Bank 1
P1296	Injector Multiple Faults - Bank 2
P1297	Injector High Side Switches Shorted Together
P1298	Injector Driver Module Failure
P1299	Cylinder Head Overtemperature Protection Active
P1300	Boost Calibration Fault
P1301	Boost Calibration High
P1302	Boost Calibration Low
P1303	Exhaust Gas Recirculation Calibration Fault
P1304	Exhaust Gas Recirculation Calibration High
P1305	Exhaust Gas Recirculation Calibration Low
P1306	Kickdown Relay Pull-in Circuit
P1307	Kickdown Relay Hold Circuit
P1309	Misfire Monitor Hardware - CMP Misaligned, CKP/CMP Noise, PCM AICE Chip
P1310	Ionization Misfire Detection Module Fault
P1311	Ionization Misfire Detection Module Communication Fault
P1316	IDM Codes Detected
P1317	Injector Circuit/IDM Codes Not Retrieved
P1340	Camshaft Position Sensor B Circuit
P1351	Ignition Diagnostic Monitor Input Circuit
P1352	Ignition Coil A Primary Circuit
P1353	Ignition Coil B Primary Circuit

FORD

P1354	Ignition Coil C Primary Circuit
P1355	Ignition Coil D Primary Circuit
P1356	Ignition Diagnostic Monitor Indicates Engine Not Turning
P1357	Ignition Diagnostic Monitor Pulsewidth Not Defined
P1358	Ignition Diagnostic Monitor Signal Out Of Self Test Range (no CPU OK)
P1359	Spark Output Circuit
P1360	Ignition Coil A Secondary Circuit
P1361	Ignition Coil B Secondary Circuit
P1362	Ignition Coil C Secondary Circuit
P1363	Ignition Coil D Secondary Circuit
P1364	Ignition Coil Primary Circuit
P1365	Ignition Coil Secondary Circuit
P1366 ... P1368	Ignition Spare
P1369	Engine Temperature Light Circuit
P1380	Camshaft Position Actuator Circuit (Bank 1)
P1381	Camshaft Position Timing Over Advanced (Bank 1)
P1383	Camshaft Position Timing Over Retarded (Bank 1)
P1385	Camshaft Position Actuator Circuit (Bank 2)
P1386	Camshaft Position Timing Over Advanced (Bank 2)
P1388	Camshaft Position Timing Over Retarded (Bank 2)
P1389	Glow Plug Circuit High Side, Low Input
P1390	Octane Adjust Service Pin In Use/Circuit Open
P1391	Glow Plug Circuit Low Input (Bank 1)
P1392	Glow Plug Circuit High Input (Bank 1)

FORD

P1393	Glow Plug Circuit Low Input (Bank 2)
P1394	Glow Plug Circuit High Input (Bank 2)
P1395	Glow Plug Monitor Fault (Bank 1)
P1396	Glow Plug Monitor Fault (Bank 2)
P1397	System Voltage Out Of Self Test Range
P1399	Glow Plug Circuit High Side, High Input
P1400	Differential Pressure Feedback EGR Circuit Low Input
P1401	Differential Pressure Feedback EGR Circuit High Input
P1402	Exhaust Gas Recirculation Metering Orifice Restricted
P1403	Differential Pressure Feedback Sensor Hoses Reversed
P1404	EGR Temperature Sensor Circuit
P1405	Differential Pressure Feedback Sensor Upstream Hose Off Or Plugged
P1406	Differential Pressure Feedback Sensor Downstream Hose Off Or Plugged
P1407	Exhaust Gas Recirculation No Flow Detected
P1408	Exhaust Gas Recirculation Flow Out Of Self Test Range
P1409	EGR Vacuum Regulator Solenoid Circuit
P1410	Auxiliary Air Cleaner Inlet Control Circuit
P1411	Secondary Air Injection Incorrect Downstream Flow Detected
P1413	Secondary Air Injection Monitor Circuit Low Input
P1414	Secondary Air Injection Monitor Circuit High Input
P1431	Misfire Monitor Disabled, unable to learn trigger wheel profile
P1442	Evaporative Emission Control System Control Leak Detected
P1443	Evaporative Emission Control System Control Valve
P1444	Purge Flow Sensor Circuit Low Input
P1445	Purge Flow Sensor Circuit High Input

FORD

P1450	Unable to Bleed Up Fuel Tank Vacuum
P1451	Evaporative Emission Control System Vent Control Circuit
P1452	Unable to Bleed Up Fuel Tank Vacuum
P1455	Evaporative Emission Control System Control Leak Detected (gross leak/no flow)
P1457	Unable To Pull Fuel Tank Vacuum
P1460	Wide Open Throttle A/C Cutout Circuit
P1461	A/C Pressure Sensor Circuit High Input
P1462	A/C Pressure Sensor Circuit Low Input
P1463	A/C Pressure Sensor Insufficient Pressure Change
P1464	A/C Demand Out Of Self Test Range
P1465	A/C Relay Circuit
P1466	A/C Refrigerant Temperature Sensor Circuit
P1469	Rapid A/C Cycling
P1473	Fan Circuit Open (VLCM)
P1474	Fan Control Primary Circuit
P1479	High Fan Control Primary Circuit
P1480	Fan Secondary Low With Low Fan On
P1481	Fan Secondary Low With High Fan On
P1482	SCP
P1483	Fan Circuit Shorted To Ground (VLCM)
P1484	Fan Driver Circuit Open To Power Ground (VLCM)
P1485	Brake Pedal Input Short To Battery
P1500	Vehicle Speed Sensor
P1501	Vehicle Speed Sensor Out Of Self Test Range
P1502	Vehicle Speed Sensor Intermittent

FORD

P1504	Idle Air Control Circuit
P1505	Idle Air Control System At Adaptive Clip
P1506	Idle Air Control Overspeed Error
P1507	Idle Air Control Underspeed Error
P1512	Intake Manifold Runner Control Stuck Closed (Bank 1)
P1513	Intake Manifold Runner Control Stuck Closed (Bank 2)
P1516	Intake Manifold Runner Control Input Error (Bank 1)
P1517	Intake Manifold Runner Control Input Error (Bank 2)
P1518	Intake Manifold Runner Control Stuck Open (Bank 1)
P1519	Intake Manifold Runner Control Stuck Closed (Bank 2)
P1520	Intake Manifold Runner Control Control Circuit
P1530	A/C Clutch Circuit Open (VLCM)
P1531	Invalid Test - Accelerator Pedal Movement
P1532	Intake Manifold Communication Control Control Circuit (Bank 2)
P1533	Air Assisted Injector Circuit
P1534	Restraint Deployment Indicator Circuit
P1536	Parking Brake Switch Circuit
P1537	Intake Manifold Runner Control Stuck Open (Bank 1)
P1538	Intake Manifold Runner Control Stuck Open (Bank 2)
P1539	A/C Clutch Circuit Overcurrent/Short (VLCM)
P1542	Primary PCM ID Circuit (dual PCM application)
P1549	Intake Manifold Communication Control Control Circuit (Bank 1)
P1550	Power Steering Pressure Sensor Out Of Self Test Range
P1565	Speed Control Command Switch Out Of Range High
P1566	Speed Control Command Switch Out Of Range Low

FORD

P1567	Speed Control Output Circuit
P1568	Speed Control Unable to Hold Speed
P1572	Brake Pedal Switch Circuit
P1573	Throttle Position Not Available
P1574	Throttle Position Sensor Outputs Disagree
P1575	Pedal Position Out Of Self Test Range
P1576	Pedal Position Not Available
P1577	Pedal Position Sensor Outputs Disagree
P1578	ETC Power Less Than Demand
P1579	ETC In Power Limiting Mode
P1580	Electronic Throttle Monitor PCM Override
P1581	Electronic Throttle Monitor Malfunction
P1582	Electronic Throttle Monitor Data Available
P1583	Electronic Throttle Monitor Cruise Disablement
P1584	Throttle Control Detected ETB Malfunction
P1585	Throttle Control Malfunction
P1586	Electronic Throttle to PCM Communication Error
P1587	Throttle Control Modulated Command Malfunction
P1588	Throttle Control Detected Loss Of Return Spring
P1589	Throttle Control Unable To Control To Desired Throttle Angle
P1600	Loss Of KAM Power, Circuit Open
P1605	Keep Alive Memory Test Failure
P1610 ... P1620	SBDS Interactive Codes
P1625	Fan Driver Circuit Open to Power B+ (VLCM)

FORD

P1626	A/C Circuit Open to Power B+ (VLCM)
P1633	Keep Alive Power Voltage Too Low
P1634	Data Output Link Circuit
P1635	Tire/Axle Out of Acceptable Range
P1636	Inductive Signature Chip Communication Error
P1639	Vehicle ID Block Corrupted, Not Programmed
P1640	Powertrain DTCs Available In Another Control Module (Ref. PID 0946)
P1641	Fuel Pump Primary Circuit
P1642	CAN Link Circuit
P1643	CAN Link Engine Control Module/Transmission Control Module Circuit/Network
P1644	Fuel Pump Speed Control Circuit
P1650	Power Steering Pressure Switch Out Of Self Test Range
P1651	Power Steering Pressure Switch Input
P1656	CAN Link PCM/PCM Circuit/Network
P1657	CAN Link Chip Malfunction
P1660	Output Circuit Check Circuit High Input
P1661	Output Circuit Check Circuit Low Input
P1662	EDU_EN Output Circuit
P1663	Fuel Demand Command Signal Output Circuit
P1667	Cylinder ID Circuit
P1668	PCM/IDM Communications Error
P1670	Electronic Feedback Signal Not Detected
P1690	Wastegate Solenoid Circuit
P1700	Transmission Indeterminate Failure (Failed to Neutral)
P1701	Reverse Engagement Error

FORD

P1702	Transmission Range Sensor Circuit Intermittent
P1703	Brake Switch Out Of Self Test Range
P1704	Transmission Range Circuit Not Indicating Park/Neutral During Self Test
P1705	Transmission Range Circuit Not Indicating Park/Neutral During Self Test
P1706	High Vehicle Speed Observed in Park
P1707	Transfer Case Neutral Indicator Hard Fault Present
P1709	Park Neutral Position Switch Out Of Self Test Range
P1711	Transmission Fluid Temperature Sensor Out Of Self Test Range
P1712	Transmission Torque Reduction Request Signal
P1713	Transmission Fluid Temperature Sensor In Range Failure
P1714	Shift Solenoid A Inductive Signature
P1715	Shift Solenoid B Inductive Signature
P1716	Shift Solenoid C Inductive Signature
P1717	Shift Solenoid D Inductive Signature
P1718	Transmission Fluid Temperature Sensor In Range Failure
P1725	Insufficient Engine Speed Increase During Self Test
P1726	Insufficient Engine Speed Decrease During Self Test
P1727	Coast Clutch Solenoid Inductive Signature
P1728	Transmission Slip
P1729	4x4L Switch
P1731	1-2 Shift Malfunction
P1732	2-3 Shift Malfunction
P1733	3-4 Shift Malfunction
P1740	Torque Converter Clutch Solenoid Inductive Signature
P1741	Torque Converter Clutch Solenoid Control Error

FORD

P1742	Torque Converter Clutch Solenoid Circuit Failed On
P1743	Torque converter clutch solenoid circuit fault
P1744	Torque Converter Clutch Solenoid Circuit Performance
P1746	Pressure Control Solenoid A Open Circuit
P1747	Pressure Control Solenoid A Short Circuit
P1748	Pressure Control Solenoid A
P1749	Pressure Control Solenoid A Failed Low
P1751	Shift Solenoid A Performance
P1754	Coast Clutch Solenoid Circuit
P1756	Shift Solenoid B Performance
P1760	Pressure Control Solenoid A Short Circuit Intermittent
P1761	Shift Solenoid C Performance
P1762	Overdrive Band Failed Off
P1766	Shift Solenoid D Performance
P1767	Torque Converter Clutch Circuit
P1768	Performance/Normal/Winter Mode Input
P1770	Clutch Solenoid Circuit
P1779	TCIL Circuit
P1780	Transmission Control Switch (O/D Cancel) Circuit Out Of Self Test Range
P1781	4X4L Circuit Out Of Self Test Range
P1782	Performance/Economy Switch Circuit Out Of Self Test Range
P1783	Transmission Overtemperature Condition
P1784	Transmission Mechanical Failure - First And Reverse
P1785	Transmission Mechanical Failure - First And Second
P1786	3-2 Downshift Error

FORD

P1787	2-1 Downshift Error
P1788	Pressure Control Solenoid B Open Circuit
P1789	Pressure Control Solenoid B Short Circuit
P1795	Inconsistent CAN Level
P1804	4-Wheel Drive High Indicator Circuit Open or Shorted To Ground
P1806	4-Wheel Drive High Indicator Short To Battery
P1808	4-Wheel Drive Low Indicator Circuit Open or Short To Ground
P1810	4-Wheel Drive Low Indicator Short To Battery
P1812	4-Wheel Drive Mode Select Switch Circuit Open
P1815	4-Wheel Drive Mode Select Switch Circuit Short To Ground
P1819	Neutral Safety Switch Input Short To Ground
P1820	Transfer Case LO To HI Shift Relay Circuit Open Or Short To Ground
P1822	Transfer Case LO To HI Shift Relay Coil Short To Battery
P1824	4-Wheel Drive Electric Clutch Relay Open Or Short To Ground
P1826	4-Wheel Drive Electric Clutch Relay Short To Battery
P1828	Transfer Case HI To LO Shift Relay Coil Circuit Open Or Short To Ground
P1830	Transfer Case HI To LO Shift Relay Coil Circuit Short To Battery
P1832	Transfer Case 4-Wheel Drive Solenoid Circuit Open or Short To Ground
P1834	Transfer Case 4-Wheel Drive Solenoid Circuit Short To Battery
P1838	No Shift Motor Movement Detected
P1846	Transfer Case Contact Plate 'A' Circuit Open
P1850	Transfer Case Contact Plate 'B' Circuit Open
P1854	Transfer Case Contact Plate 'C' Circuit Open
P1858	Transfer Case Contact Plate 'D' Circuit Open
P1866	Transfer Case Can't Be Shifted

FORD

P1867	Transfer Case Contact Plate General Circuit Failure
P1876	Transfer Case 2-Wheel Drive Solenoid Circuit Open Or Short To Ground
P1877	Transfer Case 2-Wheel Drive Solenoid Circuit Short To Battery
P1881	Engine Coolant Level Switch Circuit
P1882	Engine Coolant Level Switch Circuit Short To Ground
P1883	Engine Coolant Level Switch Circuit
P1884	Engine Coolant Level Lamp Circuit Short To Ground
P1891	Transfer Case Contact Plate Ground Return Open Circuit
P1900	Output Shaft Speed Sensor Circuit Intermittent
P1901	Turbine Shaft Speed Sensor Circuit Intermittent
P1902	Kickdown Solenoid Relay Control Circuit
P1903	Kickdown Solenoid Circuit Low Voltage
P1904	Kickdown Solenoid Circuit High Voltage
U1021	SCP (J1850) Invalid or Missing Data for Air Conditioning Clutch Sense Input
U1039	SCP (J1850) Invalid or Missing Data for Vehicle Speed
U1051	SCP (J1850) Invalid or Missing Data for Brake Input
U1073	SCP (J1850) Invalid or Missing Data for Engine Coolant Fan Status
U1075	SCP (J1850) Invalid or Missing Data for Engine Oil Temperature
U1131	SCP (J1850) Invalid or Missing Data for Fuel Pump Status
U1135	SCP (J1850) Invalid or Missing Data for Ignition Switch / Starter
U1451	SCP (J1850) Invalid or Missing Data From Anti-Theft Module, Vehicle Immobilized

OBD II FAULT CODES

GEO

P1250	Early fuel evaporation heater circuit fault
P1300	Ignition Coil 1 Primary Feedback Circuit
P1305	Ignition Coil 2 Primary Feedback Circuit
P1310	Ignition Coil 3 Primary Feedback Circuit
P1315	Ignition Coil 4 Primary Feedback Circuit
P1335	Crankshaft position sensor circuit
P1346	Intake Camshaft Position System Performance
P1349	Intake Camshaft Position System
P1408	MAP Sensor Circuit
P1410	Fuel tank pressure system fault
P1450	Barometric pressure sensor circuit fault
P1451	Barometric pressure sensor performance
P1460	Cooling fan control system fault
P1500	Starter signal circuit fault
P1510	Backup power supply fault
P1520	Stop Lamp Switch Circuit
P1530	Ignition timing adjustment switch circuit
P1600	PCM battery circuit fault
P1656	Intake CMP Actuator Solenoid Control Circuit

OBD II FAULT CODES

GM (Buick/Cadillac/Chevrolet/GMC/Oldsmobile/Pontiac/Saturn)

B0001	PCM Discrete Input Speed Signal Error
B0004	PCM Discrete Input Speed Signal Not Present
B0005	In Park Switch Circuit Malfunction
B0016	Passenger Frontal Deployment Loop Resistance Low
B0017	Passenger Frontal Deployment Loop Open
B0018	Passenger Frontal Deployment Loop Voltage Out of Range
B0022	Driver Frontal Deployment Loop Resistance Low
B0024	Driver Frontal Deployment Loop Voltage Out of Range
B0026	Driver Frontal Deployment Loop Open
B0028	RF Side Deployment Loop Resistance Low
B0029	RF Side Deployment Loop Open
B0030	RF Side Deployment Loop Voltage Out of Range
B0035	ADS Closed/Shorted to Ground
B0036	ADS Open/Missing/Shorted to Battery
B0037	AUX switch closed/shorted to ground
B0038	AUX switch open/shorted to battery
B0040	LF Side Deployment Loop Resistance Low
B0041	LF Side Deployment Loop Open
B0045	LF Side Deployment Loop Voltage Out of Range
B0051	Deployment Commanded
B0053	Deployment Commanded With Loop Faults Present
B0057	RF Pretensioner Deployment Loop Resistance Low
B0058	RF Pretensioner Deployment Loop Open
B0059	RF Pretensioner Deployment Loop Voltage Out of Range
B0064	LF Pretensioner Deployment Loop Resistance Low

OBD II FAULT CODES

GM (Buick/Cadillac/Chevrolet/GMC/Oldsmobile/Pontiac/Saturn)

B0065	LF Pretensioner Deployment Loop Open
B0066	LF Pretensioner Deployment Loop Voltage Out of Range
B0073	Supplemental deployment loop #1 resistance low
B0074	Supplemental deployment loop #1 open
B0075	Supplemental deployment loop #1 short to ground/voltage out of range
B0077	LF SIS malfunction
B0078	RF SIS malfunction
B0079	Incorrect LF SIS installed
B0080	Discard LF SIS
B0081	Incorrect RF SIS installed
B0082	Discard RF SIS
B0086	Supplemental Deployment Loop #2 Resistance Low
B0087	Supplemental deployment loop #2 open
B0088	Supplemental deployment loop #2 short to ground/voltage out of range
B0090	Active switch voltage out of range
B0091	Active switch: wrong state
B0092	PPS passenger detection error
B0093	PPS/CPS self-test malfunction
B0094	CPS childseat detection error
B0095	SDM-PPS/CPS mismatch malfunction
B0126	Right Panel Discharge Temperature Fault
B0131	Right Heater Discharge Temperature Fault
B0159	Outside Temp Sensor Failure
B0164	In-Car Temp Sensor Failure (driver)
B0169	In-car Temp Sensor Failure (passenger -not used)

GM (Buick/Cadillac/Chevrolet/GMC/Oldsmobile/Pontiac/Saturn)

B0174	Left Panel Discharge Temperature Fault
B0179	Left Heater Discharge Temperature Fault
B0184	Left Solar Sensor Fault
B0189	Right Solar Sensor Fault
B0234	Air Mix Door #1 (driver) Range Error
B0237	Air Mix Door #1 Inoperative Error
B0248	Mode Door Inoperative Error
B0249	HTR/DEF/A/C Door Range Error
B0252	HTR/DEF/A/C Door Inoperative Error
B0268	A/I Door Inoperative Error
B0269	A/I Door Range Error
B0272	A/I Door Inoperative Error
B0279	Air Mix Door #2 (Passenger) Range Error
B0282	Air Mix Door #2 Inoperative Error
B0285	Electric Rear Defrost Circuit Low
B0286	Electric Rear Defrost Circuit High
B0332	Outside Temp Sensor Circuit Short to Ground
B0333	Outside Temp Sensor Open
B0337	Inside Temp Sensor Circuit Short to Ground
B0338	Inside Temp Sensor Open
B0348	Sun Load Temp Sensor Circuit Open
B0361	Motor 1 Feedback Short
B0363	Motor 1 Feedback Open
B0365	Motor 2 Feedback Short
B0367	Motor 2 Feedback Open

OBD II FAULT CODES

GM (Buick/Cadillac/Chevrolet/GMC/Oldsmobile/Pontiac/Saturn)

B0408	Air Mix Door #1 (driver) Inoperative Error
B0409	Air Mix Door #1 (driver) Range Error
B0419	Air Mix Door #2 (passenger) Range Error
B0423	Air Mix Door #2 (passenger) Inoperative Error
B0428	Air Mix Door #3 (rear) Inoperative Error
B0429	Air Mix Door #3 (rear) Range Error
B0432	Rear Defog Relay Open Or Short To Ground
B0433	Rear Defog Relay Circuit Short To Voltage/Internal Open
B0441	LH Mix Motor Out of Range
B0446	RH Mix Motor Out of Range
B0490	Passenger Temperature Control 'Cooler' Switch Stuck Range
B0502	RH DRL Relay Circuit (Open or Short to Ground)
B0503	RH DRL Relay Circuit (Short to Voltage or BCM Internal Open)
B0507	LH DRL Relay Circuit (Open or Short to Ground)
B0508	LH DRL Relay Circuit (Short to Voltage or BCM Internal Open)
B0510	Right Panel Discharge Temperature Sensor Failure
B0515	Right Heater Discharge Temperature Sensor Failure
B0516	VSS Signal Out Of Range
B0520	Rear Discharge Temperature Sensor Failure
B0521	TACH Signal Out Of Range
B0530	Fuel Sender Stuck
B0532	Fuel Sender Shorted To Ground
B0533	Fuel Sender Open or Shorted to Battery
B0561	Tach Data Out of Range
B0566	Infl Rest System Indicator Circuit Malf

GM (Buick/Cadillac/Chevrolet/GMC/Oldsmobile/Pontiac/Saturn)

B0570	Season Odometer Malfunction
B0600	Option Content Failure
B0602	PLL Oscillator Error
B0603	Write Error
B0605	Internal Memory Malfunction
B0607	RFA Internal Fault
B0608	Power Moding Error
B0670	Internal IPC Malfunction
B0680	Passenger Air Bag Disabled Indicator Circuit Malfunction
B0686	Security System Indicator Circuit range / performance (over current)
B0687	Security System Indicator Circuit Low
B0688	Security System Indicator Circuit High
B0689	Security system indicator circuit open
B0702	RAP Relay Open or Short to Ground
B0703	RAP Relay Short to B+
B0768	Service AWD/4WD Indicator Circuit High
B0802	Brake To Shift Indicator Short To Ground
B0803	Brake To Shift Indicator Short To Battery
B0807	Inadvertent Power Or Battery 3 Short To Ground
B0812	Battery Power 3 Open
B0827	Traction Control LED Circuit Low
B0828	Traction Control LED Circuit High
B0835	Ignition 1 Malfunction
B0846	5 Volt Feed
B0851	Clean Battery Out Of Range

OBD II FAULT CODES

GM (Buick/Cadillac/Chevrolet/GMC/Oldsmobile/Pontiac/Saturn)

B0856	Dirty Battery
B0860	Device Ignition Start Circuit Malfunction
B0862	Voltage Regulator Malfunction
B0931	Compass Sensor Circuit Malfunction
B0936	Low Coolant Indicated
B0938	Coolant Level Sensor Shorted to Ground
B0940	Coolant Level Sensor Open/Not Connected
B1000	ECU Malfunction
B1001	Option Configuration Error
B1003	RFA Programming Message Not Received
B1004	Loss of Keep Alive Memory
B1005	KAM Malfunction
B1007	EEPROM Write Error
B1009	EEPROM checksum error
B1011	RAM Malfunction
B1013	ROM Checksum Error
B1014	Program ROM CheckSum Error
B1016	Passenger Deployment loop resistance low
B1017	Passenger Deployment loop open
B1018	Passenger Deployment Loop Voltage Out of Range
B1022	Driver Deployment loop resistance low
B1024	Driver Deployment Loop Voltage Out of Range
B1026	Driver Deployment loop open
B1035	ADS Shorted To Ground Or ADS Stuck Closed
B1036	ADS Missing Or Shorted To Voltage

GM (Buick/Cadillac/Chevrolet/GMC/Oldsmobile/Pontiac/Saturn)

B1051	Deployment Commanded
B1053	Deployment Commanded With Loop Malfunction
B1060	Temperature Sensor Circuit Low
B1061	Lamp Circuit Failure
B1062	Temperature Sensor Circuit Open
B1071	Internal SDM Failure
B1093	Loop Reserve Voltage High
B1115	Passenger Deployment loop resistance high
B1116	Passenger Deployment loop resistance low
B1117	Passenger Deployment loop open
B1121	Driver Deployment loop resistance high
B1122	Driver Deployment loop resistance low
B1124	Driver or Passenger Deployment Loop Short to Ground
B1125	Driver or Passenger Deployment Loop Short to Voltage
B1126	Driver Deployment loop open
B1128	Driver Side Bag LPS Missing / LPS Short To Voltage / Low Pressure
B1129	Passenger Side Bag LPS Short To Voltage
B1130	Passenger Side Bag LPS Missing / LPS Short To Voltage / Low Pressure
B1131	Passenger Pretensioner Loop Resistance High
B1132	Passenger Pretensioner Loop Resistance Low
B1134	Passenger Pretensioner Loop Open
B1135	ADS Shorted To Ground Or ADS Stuck Closed
B1136	ADS Missing Or Shorted To Voltage
B1141	Driver Pretensioner Loop Resistance High
B1142	Driver Pretensioner Loop Resistance Low

OBD II FAULT CODES

GM (Buick/Cadillac/Chevrolet/GMC/Oldsmobile/Pontiac/Saturn)

B1144	Driver or Passenger Pretensioner Loop Shorted To Ground
B1145	Driver or Passenger Pretensioner Loop Shorted To Voltage
B1146	Driver Pretensioner Loop Open
B1147	Driver Side Bag System Fault
B1148	Passenger Side Bag System Fault
B1151	Deployment event detected/commanded
B1152	Event Data Recording Memory Full
B1153	Deployment Commanded With Loop Fault
B1154	Passenger Side Suppression Fault
B1155	Calibration key does not match
B1156	Deployment Commanded Pretensioner
B1159	Loss Of Serial Data - Key Not Received
B1160	Loss Of Serial Data - VIN Not Received
B1161	Primary warning lamp circuit
B1163	Loss Of Serial Data No Response For Lamp Request
B1171	Internal SDM fault
B1245	CD Changer Not Responding
B1271	Theft Lock Enabled (IRC only)
B1310	Open in outside temperature circuit
B1311	Short in outside temperature circuit
B1312	Open in A/C high side, temperature circuit
B1313	A/C high side temperature sensor short
B1314	Open in evaporator inlet, temperature circuit
B1315	Short in evaporator inlet, temperature circuit
B1316	Open in in-car temperature circuit

GM (Buick/Cadillac/Chevrolet/GMC/Oldsmobile/Pontiac/Saturn)

B1317	Short in in-car temperature circuit
B1318	Open Sun load circuit
B1319	Drivers Sun load sensor short
B1321	A/C Low side temperature sensor fault
B1324	A/C Refrigerant Over pressure
B1326	Pass. In Car Temp Sensor
B1327	Source/Battery Voltage Low
B1328	Source/Battery Voltage High
B1330	Left panel discharge sensor fault
B1331	Right panel discharge sensor fault
B1332	Left heater discharge sensor fault
B1333	Right heater discharge sensor fault
B1334	Secondary Head
B1339	Battery Power 2 Open
B1340	Air mix door #1 movement failure
B1341	Air mix door #2 movement failure
B1343	Air inlet door movement
B1344	HTR/DEF/AC Door Movement Fault
B1347	Very low A/C refrigerant warning
B1348	Very low A/C refrigerant pressure condition
B1349	GND 2 Open
B1350	Coolant overtemp condition
B1365	Ignition 0 Circuit Malfunction
B1367	Device Ignition 0 Circuit Low
B1369	Ignition 0 Input

GM (Buick/Cadillac/Chevrolet/GMC/Oldsmobile/Pontiac/Saturn)

B1372	Device Ignition 1 (ON/START) Circuit Low
B1374	Ignition 1 Input
B1379	Ignition 3 Input
B1382	Device Ignition ACC Circuit Low
B1390	Battery Voltage Sense Fault
B1396	5 Volt Feed
B1397	VCC Short to Ground
B1398	VCC Short to B+
B1399	Loss of KDD communications
B1422	Ignition Switch Problem
B1424	Device #1 Voltage Low
B1425	Device #1 Voltage High
B1438	High Voltage Output Current Draw Too High
B1440	Power Mode Master Input Circuits Mismatch
B1477	Retained Accessory Power Circuit Low
B1478	Retained Accessory Power Circuit High
B1480	Battery Rundown Protection Circuit Malfunction
B1482	Inadv. Pwr Short to Ground
B1483	Battery Rundown Protection Circuit High
B1487	Generator L-Terminal Low
B1488	Generator L-Terminal High
B1492	Generator F-Terminal Low
B1493	Generator F-Terminal High
B1507	High Power Control Circuit Low
B1508	High Power Control Circuit High

GM (Buick/Cadillac/Chevrolet/GMC/Oldsmobile/Pontiac/Saturn)

B1510	Air Bag Telltale Open
B1512	DIC Switch 1 Signal Short To Gnd
B1513	Charging System Voltage Out of Range Low
B1514	Charging System Voltage Out of Range High
B1517	DIC Switch 2 Signal Short To Gnd
B1520	Reset Switch Input Shorted to Ground
B1521	English/Metric Switch Input Shorted to Ground
B1522	DIC Fuel Switch Input Shorted to Ground
B1523	DIC Gage Switch Input Shorted to Ground
B1524	DIC Odometer Switch Input Shorted to Ground
B1527	DIC Switch 4 Signal Short To Gnd
B1532	DIC Switch 5 Signal Short To Gnd
B1537	DIC Switch 6 Signal Short To Gnd
B1542	Oil Temp Circuit Short To Gnd
B1543	Oil Temp Circuit Open
B1552	KAM reset
B1556	EEPROM error
B1557	EEPROM Calibration Error
B1558	EEPROM checksum error
B1562	Mirror Switch Right Input Stuck Low
B1563	Mirror Right Switch Stuck
B1567	Mirror Switch Left Input Stuck Low
B1568	Mirror Left Switch Stuck
B1572	Mirror Switch Up Input Stuck Low
B1573	Mirror Up Switch Stuck

OBD II FAULT CODES

GM (Buick/Cadillac/Chevrolet/GMC/Oldsmobile/Pontiac/Saturn)

B1577	Mirror Switch Down Input Stuck Low
B1578	Mirror Down Switch Stuck
B1582	Driver Mirror Horizontal Position Sensor Short to Ground
B1583	Driver Mirror Horizontal Position Sensor Short to Battery
B1586	Mirror Horizontal Position Sensor-Out of
B1591	Mirror Vertical Position Sensor-Out of Range/Open
B1592	Driver Mirror Vertical Position Sensor Short to Ground
B1593	Driver Mirror Vertical Position Sensor Short to Battery
B1612	Passenger Mirror Horizontal Position Sensor Short to Ground
B1613	Passenger Mirror Horizontal Position Sensor Short to Battery
B1622	Passenger Mirror Vertical Position Sensor Short to Ground
B1623	Passenger Mirror Vertical Position Sensor Short to Battery
B1652	KAM Reset
B1656	EEPROM Write Error
B1657	EEPROM Calibration Error
B1658	EEPROM Checksum Error
B1697	Mirror left-up control switch circuit low
B1702	Mirror left-down control switch circuit low
B1707	Mirror right-up control switch circuit low
B1710	Switched Antenna Error
B1712	Mirror right-down control switch circuit low
B1717	Mirror power fold control switch circuit low
B1720	Switched Fourteen Volt Error
B1721	Switched Internal Battery Error
B1722	Sixteen Volt Error

GM (Buick/Cadillac/Chevrolet/GMC/Oldsmobile/Pontiac/Saturn)

B1735	Front Vertical Up Switch Failed
B1740	Radio configuration problem
B1745	Rear Vertical Up Switch Failed
B1750	Rear Vertical Down Switch Failed
B1752	KAM reset
B1753	Oscillator/Watchdog/COP fault
B1755	Horizontal Forward Switch Failed
B1760	CD Changer not responding
B1761	CD Changer tracking problem
B1762	CD Changer focus problem
B1763	CD Player load/unload problem
B1770	Cassette not responding
B1771	Cassette tape speed slow
B1772	Cassette head cleaning required
B1780	Theft Lock Enabled
B1802	Inadv. Pwr Short to Ground
B1805	Ignition Switch Problem
B1815	Recline Forward Switch Failed
B1820	Recline Aft Switch Failed
B1825	Recline Sensor Failed
B1826	Lf/Driver Recline Sensor Circuit Performance
B1830	Lumbar Forward Switch Failed
B1835	Lumbar Aft Switch Failed
B1840	Lumbar Up Switch Failed
B1845	Lumbar Down Switch Failed

OBD II FAULT CODES

GM (Buick/Cadillac/Chevrolet/GMC/Oldsmobile/Pontiac/Saturn)

B1850	Lumbar Forward/Aft Sensor Failed
B1851	Lf/Driver Lumbar Horizontal Sensor Circuit Performance
B1860	Lumbar Up/Down Sensor Failed
B1861	Lf/Driver Lumbar Vertical Sensor Circuit Performance
B1870	Head Restraint Up Switch Failed
B1875	Head Restraint Down Switch Failed
B1900	Head Restraint Up/Down Sensor Failed
B1910	Generator L-terminal open circuit
B1911	Generator L-terminal fault
B1912	Heated Seat Switch-Mode Input Shorted to Ground
B1917	Heated Seat Switch-Temperature Input Shorted to Ground
B1970	Exterior lamp power failure
B1971	Inadvertant power failure
B1972	Low power output failure
B1973	High power control output failure
B1981	Battery Volts low
B1982	Battery Volts high
B1983	Battery/Source Volts low
C0000	Vehicle Speed Information Circuit Malfunction
C0021	No Vehicle Speed Signal
C0022	Solenoid Circuit Open Or Shorted
C0023	PSCM Malfunction
C0035	Left Front Wheel Speed Sensor Circuit Malfunction
C0036	Left Front Wheel Speed Circuit Range Performance
C0040	Right Front Wheel Speed Sensor Circuit Malfunction

GM (Buick/Cadillac/Chevrolet/GMC/Oldsmobile/Pontiac/Saturn)

C0041	Right Front Wheel Speed Circuit Range Performance
C0045	Left Rear Wheel Speed Sensor Circuit Malfunction
C0046	Left Rear Wheel Speed Sensor Circuit Range Performance
C0050	Right Rear Wheel Speed Sensor Circuit Malfunction
C0051	Right Rear Wheel Speed Circuit Range Performance
C0055	Rear Wheel Speed Sensor Circuit Malfunction
C0056	Rear Wheel Speed Sensor Circuit Range Performance
C0060	Left Front ABS Solenoid #1 Circuit Malfunction
C0065	Left Front ABS Solenoid #2 Circuit Malfunction
C0070	Right Front ABS Solenoid #1 Circuit Malfunction
C0075	Right Front ABS Solenoid #2 Circuit Malfunction
C0080	Left Rear ABS Solenoid #1 Circuit Malfunction
C0085	Left Rear ABS Solenoid #2 Circuit Malfunction
C0090	Right Rear ABS Solenoid #1 Circuit Malfunction
C0095	Right Rear ABS Solenoid #2 Circuit Malfunction
C0100	Vehicle Speed Information Circuit Malfunction
C0105	Rear ABS Solenoid #2 Circuit Malfuction
C0110	Pump Motor Malfunction
C0114	Pump Motor Circuit Open
C0116	Pump Motor Relay Circuit Malfunction
C0121	Valve Relay Circuit Malfunction
C0125	Valve Relay Circuit Open
C0131	ABS/TCS System Pressure Circuit Malfunction
C0132	ABS/TCS System Pressure Circuit Range Performance
C0141	Left Hand TCS Solenoid #1 Circuit Malfunction

OBD II FAULT CODES

GM (Buick/Cadillac/Chevrolet/GMC/Oldsmobile/Pontiac/Saturn)

C0146	Left Hand TCS Solenoid #2 Circuit Malfunction
C0151	Right Hand TCS Solenoid #1 Circuit Malfunction
C0156	Right Hand TCS Solenoid #2 Circuit Malfunction
C0161	ABS/TCS Brake Switch Circuit Malfunction
C0166	TCS Priming Line Valve Circuit Malfunction
C0171	TCS Pilot Valve Circuit Malfunction
C0181	Throttle Reduction Motor Circuit Malfunction
C0182	Throttle Reduction Motor Circuit Range Performance
C0186	Lateral Accelerometer Circuit Malfunction
C0187	Lateral Accelerometer Circuit Range Performance
C0196	Yaw Rate Circuit Malfunction
C0197	Yaw Rate Circuit Range Performance
C0221	Right Front Wheel Speed Sensor Circuit Open
C0222	Right Front Wheel Speed Signal Missing
C0223	Right Front Wheel Speed Signal Erratic
C0225	Left Front Wheel Speed Sensor Circuit Open
C0226	Left Front Wheel Speed Signal Missing
C0227	Left Front Wheel Speed Signal Erratic
C0229	Drop Out of Both Front Speed Sensors
C0235	Rear Wheel Speed Signal Circuit Open
C0236	TCS RPM Signal Circuit Malfunction
C0237	TCS Throttle Position Signal Malfunction
C0238	TCS Throttle Position Sensor Comparison Malfunction
C0239	TCS Spark Retard Monitoring Malfunction
C0240	PCM Traction Control Not Allowed

GM (Buick/Cadillac/Chevrolet/GMC/Oldsmobile/Pontiac/Saturn)

C0241 ... C0243	EBCM Control Valve Circuit
C0244	PWM Delivered Torque Malfunction
C0245	Wheel Speed Sensor Frequency Error
C0246 ... C0254	EBCM Control Valve Circuit
C0265	EBCM Motor Relay Circuit
C0266	Throttle Reduction Motor Controller Malfunction
C0267	Pump Motor Circuit Open
C0268	Pump Motor Circuit Shorted
C0271 ... C0273	EBCM Malfunction
C0274	Excessive Isolation Time
C0281	Stop Lamp Switch Circuit
C0284	EBCM Malfunction
C0286	ABS Indicator Lamp Circuit Shorted to Battery
C0288	Brake Warning Lamp Circuit Shorted To Battery
C0300	Rear Propshaft Signal Circuit Malfunction
C0305	Front Propshaft Speed Sensor System Malfunction
C0308	Motor A/B Circuit Low
C0309	Motor A/B Circuit High
C0310	Motor A/B Circuit Open
C0315	Motor Ground Circuit Open

OBD II FAULT CODES

GM (Buick/Cadillac/Chevrolet/GMC/Oldsmobile/Pontiac/Saturn)

C0323	Transfer Case Lock Circuit Low
C0324	Transfer Case Lock Circuit High
C0327	Encoder Circuit
C0357	Park Switch Circuit High
C0367	Front Axle Control Circuit High
C0374	General System Malfunction
C0376	Front/Rear Propshaft Speed Mismatch Detected
C0385	4WD Low Discreet Output Circuit High
C0387	Unable to complete shift
C0450	Steering Assist Control Actuator Circuit Range Performance
C0452	Steering Assist Control Solenoid Circiut Low
C0453	Steering Assist Control Solenoid Circiut High
C0455	Steering Position Sensor Circuit Malfunction
C0472	Steering Position & Rate Of Change Sensor Circuit Low
C0473	Steering Position & Rate Of Change Sensor Circuit High
C0495	EVO Tracking Error
C0498	Steering Assist Control Solenoid Feed Circuit Low
C0499	Steering Assist Control Solenoid Feed Circuit High
C0500	EVO Tracking Error
C0502	EVO Solenoid Circuit Low
C0503	EVO Solenoid Circuit High
C0504	Steering Assist Control Solenoid Return Circuit High
C0507	Steering Wheel Position Sensor Signal Voltage Low
C0508	Steering Wheel Position Sensor Signal Voltage High
C0550	ECU Malfunction

GM (Buick/Cadillac/Chevrolet/GMC/Oldsmobile/Pontiac/Saturn)

C0551	Option Configuration Error
C0559	EEPROM Checksum Error
C0563	Calibration ROM Checksum Error
C0577	LF Solenoid/Motor/Actuator Circuit Low
C0578	LF Solenoid/Motor/Actuator Circuit High
C0579	LF Solenoid/Motor/Actuator Circuit Open
C0582	RF Solenoid/Motor/Actuator Circuit Low
C0583	RF Solenoid/Motor/Actuator Circuit High
C0584	RF Solenoid/Motor/Actuator Circuit Open
C0587	LR Solenoid/Motor/Actuator Circuit Low
C0588	LR Solenoid/Motor/Actuator Circuit High
C0589	LR Solenoid/Motor/Actuator Circuit Open
C0592	RR Solenoid/Motor/Actuator Circuit Low
C0593	RR Solenoid/Motor/Actuator Circuit High
C0594	RR Solenoid/Motor/Actuator Circuit Open
C0611	V.I.N. Information Error
C0615	LF Position Sensor Circuit Malfunction
C0620	RF Position Sensor Circuit Malfunction
C0625	Level Control Suspension Sensor Malfunction
C0628	Level Control Suspension Sensor Short to B+
C0630	RR Position Sensor Circuit Malfunction
C0635	LF Normal Force Circuit Malfunction
C0638	LF Normal Force Circuit High
C0640	RF Normal Force Circuit Malfunction
C0643	RF Normal Force Circuit High

GM (Buick/Cadillac/Chevrolet/GMC/Oldsmobile/Pontiac/Saturn)

C0655	Level Control Compressor Relay Malfunction
C0657	Level Control Compressor Circuit Low
C0658	Level Control Compressor Relay Short to B+
C0660	Level Control Exhaust Valve Circuit Malfunction
C0662	Level Control Exhaust Valve Circuit Low
C0663	Level Control Exhaust Valve Short to B+
C0665	Lift/Dive Signal Circuit Malfunction
C0690	Damper Control Relay Circuit Malfunction
C0691	Damper Control Relay Circuit Range/Performance
C0693	Damper Control Relay Circuit High
C0695	Position Sensor Overcurrent (8 Volt Supply)
C0696	Position Sensor Overcurrent (5 Volt Supply)
C0697	Level Control Accessory Inflator Switch Malfunction
C0710	Steering Position Signal Malfunction
C0870	Device Voltage Reference Output 1 Circuit Malfunction
C0875	Device Voltage Reference Input 2 Circuit Malfunction
C0895	Device Voltage Malfunction
C0896	Device Voltage Range/Performance
C0899	Device #1 Voltage Low
C0900	Device #1 Voltage High
C0901	Device #2 Voltage Low
C1210	Brake Fluid Level Switch Open
C1211	ABS Warning Lamp Circuit Malfunction
C1214	Solenoid Valve Relay Contacts Open
C1217	BPMV Pump Motor Relay Contacts Circuit Open

GM (Buick/Cadillac/Chevrolet/GMC/Oldsmobile/Pontiac/Saturn)

C1221	Righ Front wheel speed sensor circuit open
C1222	Righ Front wheel speed signal missing
C1223	Righ Front wheel speed signal erratic
C1224	Right Rear Wheel Speed Sensor Input Signal Equals Zero
C1225	Left Front wheel speed sensor circuit open
C1226	Left Front wheel speed signal missing
C1227	Left Front wheel speed signal erratic
C1228	Right Rear Excessive Wheel Speed Variation
C1229	Simultaneous drop out of front wheel speed signals
C1232	Left Front Wheel Speed Sensor Circuit Open or Shorted
C1233	Right Front Wheel Speed Sensor Circuit Open or Shorted
C1234	Left Rear Wheel Speed Sensor Circuit Open or Shorted
C1235	Rear Wheel Speed Sensor Circuit Open
C1236	Rear Wheel speed signal missing
C1237	Rear Wheel speed signal erratic
C1238	Wheel speed signal malfuntion
C1241	Right Front isolation solenoid circuit open
C1242	Right Front PWM solenoid circuit open
C1243	Right Front isolation solenoid circuit shorted
C1244	Right Front PWM solenoid circuit shorted
C1245	Left Front isolation solenoid circuit open
C1246	Left Front PWM solenoid circuit open
C1247	Left Front isolation solenoid circuit shorted
C1248	Left Front PWM solenoid circuit shorted
C1251	Rear isolation solenoid circuit open

OBD II FAULT CODES

GM (Buick/Cadillac/Chevrolet/GMC/Oldsmobile/Pontiac/Saturn)

C1252	Rear PWM solenoid circuit open
C1253	Rear isolation solenoid circuit shorted
C1254	Rear PWM solenoid circuit shorted
C1255	EBTCM Internal Malfunction (ABS/TCS Disabled)
C1256	EBTCM Internal Malfunction
C1261	Left Front Hold Valve Solenoid Malfunction
C1262	Left Front Release Valve Solenoid Malfunction
C1263	Right Front Hold Valve Solenoid Malfunction
C1264	VCM/4WAL system voltage low
C1265	Pump motor relay circuit open
C1266	Pump motor relay circuit shorted
C1267	Open pump motor circuit
C1268	Pump motor stalled -or- Pump circuit shorted
C1269	VCM/4WAL voltage low during ABS stop
C1271	Left Front TCS Master Cylinder Isolation Valve Malfunction
C1272	Left Front TCS Prime Valve Malfunction
C1273	Right Front TCS Master Cylinder Isolation Valve Malfunction
C1274	Excessive isolation time
C1275	VCM history memory malfunction
C1276	Delivered Torque PWM Signal Malfunction
C1277	Requested Torque PWM Signal Malfunction
C1278	TCS Temporarily Inhibited By PCM
C1281	Brake switch circuit shorted or open
C1282	Yaw Rate Sensor Bias Circuit Malfunction
C1283	Excessive Time to Center Steering

GM (Buick/Cadillac/Chevrolet/GMC/Oldsmobile/Pontiac/Saturn)

C1284	Lateral Acceleration Sensor Self Test Malfunction
C1285	Lateral Acceleration Sensor Circuit Malfunction
C1286	Antilock indicator lamp malfunction
C1287	Steering Sensor Rate Malfunction
C1288	Steering Sensor Circuit Malfunction
C1291	Open Brake Lamp Switch Circuit During Deceleration
C1293	Open Brake Lamp Switch Circuit During Deceleration Set In Current Or Previous Ignition Cycle
C1294	Brake Lamp Switch Cricuit Always Active
C1295	Brake Light Switch Circuit Open
C1297	PCM Indicated Extended Brake Travel Malfunction
C1298	PCM Indicated Class 2 Serial Data Link Malfunction
C1300	Class 2 Shorted to Ground
C1301	Class 2 Shorted to Battery +
C1650	Controller Fault
C1658	EEPROM Calibration Fault
C1710	Left Front Strut Actuator Short to B+
C1711	Left Front Strut Actuator Short to Ground
C1712	Left Front Strut Actuator Open Circuit
C1715	Right Front Strut Actuator Short to B+
C1716	Right Front Strut Actuator Short to Ground
C1717	Right Front Strut Actuator Open Circuit
C1720	Left Rear Shock Actuator Short to B+
C1721	Left Rear Shock Actuator Short to Ground
C1722	Left Rear Shock Actuator Open Circuit
C1725	Right Rear Shock Actuator Short to B+

OBD II FAULT CODES

GM (Buick/Cadillac/Chevrolet/GMC/Oldsmobile/Pontiac/Saturn)

C1726	Right Rear Shock Actuator Short to Ground
C1727	Right Rear Shock Actuator Open Circuit
C1735	ELC Compressor Short to B+
C1736	ELC Compressor Short to Ground/Open Circuit
C1737	ELC Exhaust Valve Short to B+
C1738	ELC Exhaust Valve Short to Ground/Open circuit
C1743	Speed Signal Fault [Lost]
C1744	Lift/Dive Signal Discrete Fault
C1760	Left Front Position Sensor (Input) Fault
C1761	Right Front Position Sensor (Input) Fault
C1762	Left Rear Position Sensor (Input) Fault
C1763	Right Rear Position Sensor (Input) Fault
C1768	Position Sensor Supply Over-current
C1780	Steering Sensor (Input) Fault
C1781	Steering Sensor (Supply) Over-current
C1782	LF Normal Force Short to B+
C1783	LF Normal Force Short to Ground/Open Circuit
C1784	RF Normal Force Short to B+
C1785	RF Normal Force Short to Ground/Open Circuit
C1786	Damper Control Relay Failure
C1787	Damper Control Relay Short to Ground/Open Circuit
C1788	Damper Control Relay Short to B+
C1790	Ride Control Switch (Out Of Range)
C1791	Ride Control Switch (Contact Fault)
C1792	Loss Of Intake Air Temperature Data

GM (Buick/Cadillac/Chevrolet/GMC/Oldsmobile/Pontiac/Saturn)

P0030	HO2S Heater Control Circuit Sensor 1
P0031	HO2S Heater Circuit Low Voltage Bank 1 Sensor 1
P0032	HO2S Heater Circuit High Voltage Bank 1 Sensor 1
P0036	HO2S Heater Control Circuit Sensor 2
P0037	HO2S Heater Circuit Low Voltage Bank 1 Sensor 2
P0038	HO2S Heater Circuit High Voltage Bank 1 Sensor 2
P0050	HO2S Heater Circuit Bank 2 Sensor 1
P0051	HO2S Heater Circuit Low Voltage Bank 2 Sensor 1
P0052	HO2S Heater Circuit High Voltage Bank 2 Sensor 1
P0056	HO2S Heater Circuit Bank 2 Sensor 2
P0057	HO2S Heater Circuit Low Voltage Bank 2 Sensor 2
P0058	HO2S Heater Circuit High Voltage Bank 2 Sensor 2
P1031	HO2S Heater Current Monitor Control Circuit Sensors 1
P1032	HO2S Heater Warm Up Control Circuit Sensors 1
P1105	Secondary Vacuum Sensor Circuit
P1106	MAP Sensor Ckt. Intermittent High Voltage
P1107	MAP Sensor Ckt. Intermittent Low Voltage
P1108	BARO to MAP Sen. Ckt. Comparison Too High
P1109	Secondary Port Throttle System
P1111	IAT Sensor Ckt. Intermittent High Voltage
P1112	IAT Sensor Ckt. Intermittent Low Voltage
P1113	Intake Resonance Switchover Valve Circuit
P1114	ECT Sensor Ckt. Intermittent Low Voltage
P1115	ECT Sensor Ckt. Intermittent High Voltage
P1116	ECT Signal Unstable or Intermittent

OBD II FAULT CODES

GM (Buick/Cadillac/Chevrolet/GMC/Oldsmobile/Pontiac/Saturn)

P1117	Engine Coolant Temp. Signal Out-Of-Range Low
P1118	Engine Coolant Temp. Signal Out-Of-Range High
P1119	ECT Signal Out-Of-Range With TFT Sensor
P1120	Throttle Position Sensor 1 Ckt.
P1121	TP Sensor Ckt. Intermittent High Voltage
P1122	TP Sensor Ckt. Intermittent Low Voltage
P1125	APP System
P1130	HO2S Circuit Low Variance Bank 1 Sensor 1
P1131	HO2S Circuit Low Variance Bank 1 Sensor 2
P1132	HO2S Circuit Low Variance Bank 2 Sensor 1
P1133	HO2S Insuff. Switching Bank 1 Sensor 1
P1134	HO2S Transition Time Ratio Bank 1 Sensor 1
P1135	HO2S Lean Mean Bank 1 Sensor 1
P1136	HO2S Rich Mean Bank 1 Sensor 1
P1137	HO2S Bank 1 Sensor 2 Lean System or Low Voltage
P1138	HO2S Bank 1 Sensor 2 Rich or High Voltage
P1139	HO2S Insuff. Switching Bank 1 Sensor 2
P1140	HO2S Transition Time Ratio Bank 1 Sensor 2
P1141	HO2S Bank 1 Sensor 2 Mean Voltage Level
P1143	HO2S Bank 1 Sensor 3 Lean System or Low Voltage
P1144	HO2S Bank 1 Sensor 3 Rich or High Voltage
P1145	HO2S Cross Counts Bank 1 Sensor 3
P1153	HO2S Insuff. Switching Bank 2 Sensor 1
P1154	HO2S Transition Time Ratio Bank 2 Sensor 1
P1155	HO2S Lean Mean Bank 2 Sensor 1

GM (Buick/Cadillac/Chevrolet/GMC/Oldsmobile/Pontiac/Saturn)

P1156	HO2S Rich Mean Bank 2 Sensor 1
P1157	HO2S Bank 2 Sensor 2 Lean System or Low Voltage
P1158	HO2S Bank 2 Sensor 2 Rich or High Voltage
P1159	HO2S Cross Counts Bank 2 Sensor 2
P1161	HO2S Heater Power Stage Circuit Bank 2 Sensor 2
P1163	HO2S Bank 2 Sensor 3 Lean System or Low Voltage
P1164	HO2S Bank 2 Sensor 3 Rich or High Voltage
P1165	HO2S Cross Counts Bank 2 Sensor 3
P1170	Bank to Bank Fuel TrimOffset
P1171	Fuel System Lean During Acceleration
P1185	Engine Oil Temperature Circuit
P1186	EOT Circuit Performance
P1187	EOT Sensor Ckt. Low Voltage
P1188	EOT Sensor Ckt. High Voltage
P1189	Engine Oil Pressure Switch Circuit
P1190	Engine Vacuum Leak
P1191	Intake Air Duct Air Leak
P1200	Injector Control Circuit
P1201	(Alt. Fuel) Gas Mass Sensor Circuit Range/Performance
P1202	(Alt. Fuel) Gas Mass Sensor Circuit Low Frequency
P1203	(Alt. Fuel) Gas Mass Sensor Circuit High Frequency
P1211	Mass Air Flow Circuit Intermittent High
P1212	Mass Air Flow Circuit Intermittent Low
P1214	Injection Pump Timing Offset
P1215	Ground Fault Detection Indicated

OBD II FAULT CODES

GM (Buick/Cadillac/Chevrolet/GMC/Oldsmobile/Pontiac/Saturn)

P1216	Fuel Solenoid Response Time Too Short
P1217	Fuel Solenoid Response Time Too Long
P1218	Injection Pump Calibration Circuit
P1219	Throttle Position Sensor Reference Voltage
P1220	Throttle Position Sensor 1 Ckt.
P1221	Fuel Pump Secondary Circuit Low
P1222	Injector Control Circuit Intermittent
P1225	Injector Circuit Cylinder 2 Intermittent
P1228	Injector Circuit Cylinder 3 Intermittent
P1231	Injector Circuit Cylinder 4 Intermittent
P1234	Injector Circuit Cylinder 5 Intermittent
P1237	Injector Circuit Cylinder 6 Intermittent
P1240	Injector Circuit Cylinder 7 Intermittent
P1243	Injector Circuit Cylinder 8 Intermittent
P1245	Intake Plenum Switchover Valve
P1250	Early Fuel Evaporation Heater Circuit
P1257	Supercharger System Overboost
P1258	Engine Metal Overtemperature Protection
P1260	Last Test Failed SCC -or- Theft Detected, Vehicle Immobilized
P1270	Accelerator Pedal Position Sensor A/D Converter Error
P1271	APP Sensor 1-2 Performance
P1272	Accelerator Pedal Position Sensor 2
P1273	Accelerator Pedal Position Sensor 1
P1274	Injectors Wired Incorrectly
P1275	Accelerator Pedal Position Sensor 1 Circuit

GM (Buick/Cadillac/Chevrolet/GMC/Oldsmobile/Pontiac/Saturn)

P1276	Accelerator Pedal Position Sensor 1 Circuit Performance
P1277	Accelerator Pedal Position Sensor 1 Circuit Low Voltage
P1278	Accelerator Pedal Position Sensor 1 Circuit High Voltage
P1280	Accelerator Pedal Position Sensor 2 Circuit
P1281	Accelerator Pedal Position Sensor 2 Circuit Performance
P1282	Accelerator Pedal Position Sensor 2 Circuit Low Voltage
P1283	Accelerator Pedal Position Sensor 2 Circuit High Voltage
P1285	Accelerator Pedal Position Sensor 3 Circuit
P1286	Accelerator Pedal Position Sensor 3 Circuit Performance
P1287	Accelerator Pedal Position Sensor 3 Circuit Low Voltage
P1288	Accelerator Pedal Position Sensor 3 Circuit High Voltage
P1300	Ignitor Circuit
P1305	Ignition Coil 2 Primary Feedback Circuit
P1310	Ignition Coil 3 Primary Feedback Circuit
P1315	Ignition Coil 4 Primary Feedback Circuit
P1320	IC Module 4X Ref Circuit Intermittent, No Pulses
P1321	Electronic Ignition System Fault Line
P1322	EI System or Ignition Control Extra or Missing
P1323	24X Reference Circuit Low Frequency
P1324	Crank RPM Too Low
P1335	CKP Circuit
P1336	Crankshaft Position System Variation Not Learned
P1345	CKP / CMP Correlation
P1346	Intake Camshaft Position [CMP] Sensor System Performance
P1350	Ignition Control System

OBD II FAULT CODES

GM (Buick/Cadillac/Chevrolet/GMC/Oldsmobile/Pontiac/Saturn)

P1351	IC Circuit High Voltage
P1352	IC Output High/Pulse Detected when GND_Cyl. 2
P1353	IC Output High/Pulse Detected when GND_Cyl. 3
P1354	IC Output High/Pulse Detected when GND_Cyl. 4
P1355	IC Output High/Pulse Detected when GND_Cyl. 5
P1356	IC Output High/Pulse Detected when GND_Cyl. 6
P1357	IC Output High/Pulse Detected when GND_Cyl. 7
P1358	IC Output High/Pulse Detected when GND_Cyl. 8
P1359	Ignition Control Circuit Group A
P1360	Ignition Control Circuit Group B
P1361	IC Circuit Low Voltage
P1362	IC Cylinder 2 Not Toggling After Enable
P1363	IC Cylinder 3 Not Toggling After Enable
P1364	IC Cylinder 4 Not Toggling After Enable
P1365	IC Cylinder 5 Not Toggling After Enable
P1366	IC Cylinder 6 Not Toggling After Enable
P1367	IC Cylinder 7 Not Toggling After Enable
P1368	IC Cylinder 8 Not Toggling After Enable
P1370	IC Module 4X Ref Circuit Too Many Pulses
P1371	DI Low Resolution Circuit
P1372	Crankshaft Position Sensor Circuits Performance
P1374	3X Reference Circuit
P1375	24X Reference Circuit High Voltage
P1376	Ignition Ground Circuit
P1377	IC Module CAM Pulse To 4X Reference Pulse Comparison

GM (Buick/Cadillac/Chevrolet/GMC/Oldsmobile/Pontiac/Saturn)

P1380	EBTCM DTC Detected - Rough Road Data Unusable
P1381	Misfire Detected No EBTCM/PCM Serial Data
P1390	Wheel Speed Sensor 1 - G - Sensor Circuit
P1391	Wheel Speed Sensor 1 - G - Sensor Circuit Performance
P1392	Wheel Speed Sensor 1 - G - Sensor Circuit Low Voltage
P1393	Wheel Speed Sensor 1 - G - Sensor Circuit High Voltage
P1394	Wheel Speed Sensor 1 - G - Sensor Circuit Intermittent
P1395	Wheel Speed Sensor 2 - G - Sensor Circuit
P1396	Wheel Speed Sensor 2 - G - Sensor Circuit Performance
P1397	Wheel Speed Sensor 2 - G - Sensor Circuit Low Voltage
P1398	Wheel Speed Sensor 2 - G - Sensor Circuit High Voltage
P1399	Wheel Speed Sensor 2 - G - Sensor Circuit Intermittent
P1403	Exhaust Gas Recirculation System Valve 1
P1404	Exhaust Gas Recirculation System Valve 2
P1405	Exhaust Gas Recirculation System Valve 3
P1406	EGR Valve Pintle Position Circuit
P1407	EGR Air Intrusion in Exhaust Supply to EGR Valve
P1408	Intake Manifold Pressure Sensor Circuit
P1409	EGR Vacuum System Leak
P1410	Fuel Tank Pressure System
P1415	AIR System Bank 1
P1416	AIR System Bank 2
P1418	Secondary Air Injection System Relay A Control Circuit High
P1420	Intake Air Low Pressure Switch Circuit Low Voltage
P1421	Intake Air Low Pressure Switch Circuit High Voltage

OBD II FAULT CODES

GM (Buick/Cadillac/Chevrolet/GMC/Oldsmobile/Pontiac/Saturn)

P1423	Intake Air High Pressure Switch Circuit High Voltage
P1431	Fuel Level Sensor 2 Circuit Performance
P1432	Fuel Level Sensor 2 Circuit Low Voltage
P1433	Fuel Level Sensor 2 Circuit High Voltage
P1441	EVAP System Flow During Non-Purge
P1442	EVAP Vacuum Switch High Voltage During Ignition On
P1450	Barometric pressure sensor circuit
P1451	Barometric pressure sensor performance
P1460	Cooling Fan Control System
P1480	Cooling Fan 1 Control Circuit High
P1483	Engine Cooling System Performance
P1500	Starter Signal Circuit
P1501	Vehicle Speed Sensor Circuit Intermittent
P1502	Theft Deterrent System - No Password Received
P1503	Theft Deterrent System - Password Incorrect
P1504	Vehicle Speed Output Circuit
P1508	IAC System Low RPM
P1509	IAC System High RPM
P1510	Back Up Power Supply
P1511	Throttle Control System - Backup System Performance
P1514	Airflow to TP Sensor Correlation High
P1515	Electronic Throttle System Throttle Position
P1516	Electronic Throttle Module Throttle Position
P1517	Electronic Throttle Module
P1518	Electronic Throttle Module to PCM Communication

GM (Buick/Cadillac/Chevrolet/GMC/Oldsmobile/Pontiac/Saturn)

P1519	Electronic Throttle Module Low Volts Communication Disable
P1520	Gear Indicator System
P1521	Transmission Engaged at High Throttle Angle
P1522	Park/Neutral to Drive/Reverse at High RPM
P1523	Electronic Throttle Control Throttle Return
P1524	TP Sensor Learned Cl. Throttle Angle fl Out of Range
P1525	Throttle Body ServiceRequired
P1526	TP Sensor Learn Not Complete
P1527	Transmission Range/Pressure Switch Comparison
P1528	Governor
P1529	Heated Windshield Request Problem
P1530	Ignition Timing Adjustment Switch Circuit
P1531	A/C Low Side Temperature Sensor Fault
P1532	A/C Evaporator Temperature Sensor Circuit Low Voltage
P1533	A/C Evaporator Temperature Sensor Circuit High Voltage
P1534	A/C High Side Temp. Sensor Low Voltage
P1535	A/C High Side Temperature Sensor Circuit
P1536	A/C System - ECT Overtemperature
P1537	A/C Request Circuit Low Voltage
P1538	A/C Request Circuit High Voltage
P1539	A/C Clutch Status Circuit High Voltage
P1540	A/C System High Pressure
P1541	A/C High Side Over Temperature
P1542	A/C System High Pressure High Temperature
P1543	A/C System Performance

OBD II FAULT CODES

GM (Buick/Cadillac/Chevrolet/GMC/Oldsmobile/Pontiac/Saturn)

P1544	A/C Refrigerant Condition Very Low
P1545	A/C Clutch Relay Control Circuit
P1546	A/C Clutch Status Circuit Low Voltage
P1547	A/C System Performance Degraded
P1548	A/C Recirculation Circuit
P1554	Cruise Engaged Circuit High Voltage
P1555	Electronic Variable Orifice Output
P1558	Cruise Control Servo Indicates Low
P1559	Cruise Control Power Management Mode
P1560	Cruise Control System - Transaxle Not In Drive
P1561	Cruise Vent Solenoid
P1562	Cruise Vacuum Solenoid
P1563	Cruise Vehicle Speed/Set Speed Difference Too High
P1564	Cruise Control System - Vehicle Accel. Too High
P1565	Cruise Servo Position Sensor
P1566	Cruise Control System - Engine RPM Too High
P1567	Cruise Control System - Active Braking Control Active
P1568	Cruise Servo Stroke Greater than Commanded in Cruise
P1569	Cruise Servo Stroke High While not in Cruise
P1570	Cruise Control System - Traction Control Active
P1571	TCS PWM Circuit No Frequency
P1572	ASR Active Circuit Low Too Long
P1573	PCM/EBTCM Serial Data Circuit
P1574	EBTCM System - Stop Lamp Switch Circuit High Voltage
P1575	Extended Travel Brake Switch Circuit High Voltage

GM (Buick/Cadillac/Chevrolet/GMC/Oldsmobile/Pontiac/Saturn)

P1576	BBV Sensor Circuit High Voltage
P1577	BBV Sensor Circuit Low Voltage
P1578	BBV Sensor Circuit Low Vacuum
P1579	P/N to D/R At High Throttle Angle
P1580	Cruise Move Circuit Low Voltage
P1581	Cruise Move Circuit High Voltage
P1582	Cruise Direction Circuit Low Voltage
P1583	Cruise Direction CircuitHigh Voltage
P1584	Cruise Control Disabled
P1585	Cruise Inhibit Control Circuit
P1586	Cruise Control Brake Switch 2 Circuit
P1587	Cruise Control Clutch Control Circuit Low
P1588	Cruise Control Clutch Control Circuit High
P1599	Engine Stall Or Near Stall Detected
P1600	PCM Battery
P1601	Serial Communication Problem With Device 1
P1602	Loss Of EBTCM Serial Data
P1603	Loss Of SDM Serial Data
P1604	Loss Of IPC Serial Data
P1605	Loss Of HVAC Serial Data
P1606	Serial Communication Problem With Device 6
P1607	Serial Communication Problem With Device 7
P1608	Serial Communication Problem With Device 8
P1609	Loss Of TCS Serial Data
P1610	Loss Of PZM Serial Data

OBD II FAULT CODES

GM (Buick/Cadillac/Chevrolet/GMC/Oldsmobile/Pontiac/Saturn)

P1611	Loss Of CVRTD Serial Data
P1612	Loss of IPM Serial Data
P1613	Loss of DIM Serial Data
P1614	Loss of RIM Serial Data
P1615	Loss of VTD Serial Data
P1617	Engine Oil Level Switch Circuit
P1619	Engine Oil Life Monitor Reset Circuit
P1620	Low Coolant Circuit
P1621	PCM Memory Performance
P1622	Cylinder Select
P1623	Transmission Temp Pull-Up Resistor
P1624	Customer Snapshot Data Available
P1625	PCM System Reset
P1626	Theft Deterrent System Fuel Enable Circuit
P1627	A/D Performance
P1628	ECT Pull-Up Resistor
P1629	Theft Deterrent System - Cranking Signal
P1630	Theft Deterrent System - PCM In Learn Mode
P1631	Theft Deterrent Sys. - Password Incorrect
P1632	Theft Deterrent System - Fuel disabled
P1633	Ignition Suppl. Power Circuit Low Voltage
P1634	Ignition 1 Power Circuit Low Voltage
P1635	5 Volt Reference Low
P1636	PCM Stack Overrun
P1637	Generator L-Terminal Circuit

GM (Buick/Cadillac/Chevrolet/GMC/Oldsmobile/Pontiac/Saturn)

P1638	Generator F-Terminal Circuit
P1639	5 Volt Reference 2 Circuit
P1640	Driver 1 - Input High Voltage
P1641	FC Relay 1 Control Circuit
P1642	FC Relay 2 and 3 Control Circuit
P1643	Engine Speed Output Circuit
P1644	TP Output Circuit
P1645	EVAP Solenoid Output Circuit
P1646	Driver 1 Line 6
P1647	Driver 1 Line 7
P1650	Driver 2 - Input High Voltage
P1651	Fan 1 Relay Control Circuit
P1652	VSS Output Circuit
P1653	Oil Level Lamp Control Circuit
P1654	Service Throttle Soon Lamp Control Circuit
P1655	EVAP Purge Solenoid Control Circuit
P1656	Driver 2 Line 6
P1657	1-4 Upshift Solenoid Control Circuit
P1658	Starter Enable Relay Control Circuit
P1660	Cooling Fans Control Circuit
P1661	MIL Control Circuit
P1662	Cruise Control Inhibit Control Circuit
P1663	Oil Life Lamp Control Circuit
P1664	1-4 Upshift Lamp Control Circuit
P1665	Driver 3 Line 5

OBD II FAULT CODES

GM (Buick/Cadillac/Chevrolet/GMC/Oldsmobile/Pontiac/Saturn)

P1666	Driver 3 Line 6
P1667	Reverse Inhibit Solenoid Control Circuit
P1669	ABS Unit Expected
P1670	Driver 4
P1671	Driver 4 Line 1
P1672	Low Engine Oil Level Lamp Control Circuit
P1673	Engine Hot Lamp Control Circuit
P1674	Tachometer Control Circuit
P1675	EVAP Vent Solenoid Control Circuit
P1676	Driver 4 Line 6
P1677	Driver 4 Line 7
P1680	Driver 5
P1681	Driver 5 Line 1
P1682	Driver 5 Line 2
P1683	Driver 5 Line 3
P1684	Driver 5 Line 4
P1685	Driver 5 Line 5
P1686	Driver 5 Line 6
P1687	Driver 5 Line 7
P1689	Delivered Torque Circuit Fault
P1690	ECM Loop Overrun
P1691	Coolant Gage Circuit Low Voltage
P1692	Coolant Gage Circuit High Voltage
P1693	Tachometer Circuit Low Voltage
P1694	Tachometer Circuit High Voltage

GM (Buick/Cadillac/Chevrolet/GMC/Oldsmobile/Pontiac/Saturn)

P1695	Remote Keyless Entry Circuit Low
P1696	Remote Keyless Entry Voltage High
P1700	Transmission MIL Request
P1701	Transmission MIL Request Circuit
P1705	P/N Signal Output Circuit
P1740	Transmission Torque Reduction Request Circuit
P1743	TP Signal from ECM
P1760	TCM Supply Voltage Interrupted
P1779	Engine Torque Delivered to TCM Signal
P1780	Park/Neutral Position [PNP] Switch Circuit
P1781	Engine Torque Signal Circuit
P1790	Transmission Control Module Checksum
P1791	Transmission Control Module Loop
P1792	Transmission Control Module Reprogrammable Memory
P1793	Transmission Control Module Stack Overrun
P1795	CAN Bus - Throttle Body Position
P1800	TCM Power Control Relay Circuit - Open
P1801	Performance Selector Switch Failure
P1804	Ground Control Relay
P1810	Pressure Switch Manifold
P1811	Maximum Adapt and Long Shift
P1812	Transmission Over Temperature Condition
P1813	Torque Control
P1814	Torque Converter Overstressed
P1815	Transmission Range Switch - Start In Wrong Range

OBD II FAULT CODES

GM (Buick/Cadillac/Chevrolet/GMC/Oldsmobile/Pontiac/Saturn)

P1816	TFP Valve Position Switch - Park/Neutral With Drive Ratio
P1817	TFP Valve Position Switch - Reverse With Drive Ratio
P1818	TFP Valve Position Switch - Drive Without Drive Ratio
P1819	Internal Mode Switch - No StartWrong Range
P1820	Internal Mode Switch Circuit A - Low
P1822	Internal Mode Switch Circuit B - High
P1823	Internal Mode Switch Circuit P - Low
P1825	Internal Mode Switch - Illegal Range
P1826	Internal Mode Switch Circuit C - High
P1831	PC Solenoid Power Circuit - Low Voltage
P1833	A/T Solenoids Power Circuit - Low Voltage
P1835	Kick-Down Switch
P1836	Kick-Down Switch Failed Open
P1837	Kick-Down Switch Failed Short
P1842	1-2 Shift Solenoid Circuit - Low Voltage
P1843	1-2 Shift Solenoid Circuit - High Voltage
P1844	Torque Reduction Signal Circuit Desired By TCM
P1845	Transmission Gear Ratio Output Circuit
P1847	2-3 Shift Solenoid Circuit - High Voltage
P1850	Brake Band Apply Solenoid Circuit
P1851	Brake Band Apply Solenoid Performance
P1852	Brake Band Apply SolenoidLow Voltage
P1853	Brake Band Apply Solenoid High Voltage
P1860	TCC PWM Solenoid Circuit
P1864	Torque Converter Clutch Circuit

GM (Buick/Cadillac/Chevrolet/GMC/Oldsmobile/Pontiac/Saturn)

P1868	Transmission Fluid Life
P1870	Transmission Component Slipping
P1871	Undefined Gear Ratio
P1873	TCC Stator Temp. Switch Circuit Low
P1874	TCC Stator Temp. Switch Circuit High
P1875	4WD Low Switch Circuit
P1884	TCC Enable/Shift Light Circuit
P1886	Shift Timing Solenoid
P1887	TCC Release Switch Circuit
P1890	ECM Data Input Circuit
P1891	Throttle Position Sensor PWM Signal Low
P1892	Throttle Position Sensor PWM Signal High
P1893	Engine Torque Signal Low Voltage
P1894	Engine Torque Signal High Voltage
P1895	TCM to ECM Torque Reduction Circuit
U0715	RTT Circuit Malfunction
U0835	Power Moding Error
U1000	No State of Health From Module
U1001 ... U1015	Loss of serial communications for class 2 devices
U1016	Loss of PCM Communications
U1017 ... U1025	Loss of serial communications for class 2 devices
U1026	Loss of Class 2 Communication with ATC

OBD II FAULT CODES

GM (Buick/Cadillac/Chevrolet/GMC/Oldsmobile/Pontiac/Saturn)

U1027 ... U1037	Loss of serial communications for class 2 devices
U1038	Loss of Serial Communications for Class 2 Devices
U1039	Loss of Serial Communications for Class 2 Devices
U1040	Loss Of EBCM/EBTCM Communications
U1041	Loss Of EBCM Communication
U1042	Lost Communications with Brake/Traction Control System
U1043 ... U1055	Loss of Serial Communications for Class 2 Devices
U1056	Loss Of RTD/RSS Communications
U1057 ... U1063	Loss of Serial Communications for Class 2 Devices
U1064	Loss of Communication with BCM
U1065	Loss of IPM Communications
U1066	Loss Of RIM Communications
U1067 ... U1087	Loss of Serial Communications for Class 2 Devices
U1088	Loss Of SIR/SDM Communications
U1089 ... U1095	Loss of Serial Communications for Class 2 Devices
U1096	Loss Of IPC Communications

GM (Buick/Cadillac/Chevrolet/GMC/Oldsmobile/Pontiac/Saturn)

U1097 ... U1122	Loss of Serial Communications for Class 2 Devices
U1123 ... U1127	Loss of serial communications for class 2 devices
U1128	Loss Of IRC Communications
U1129	Loss Of AMP Communications
U1130 ... U1143	Loss of serial communications for class 2 devices
U1144	Loss Of PHN Communications
U1145	Loss Of NAV Communications
U1146	Loss Of Onstar Communiction
U1147 ... U1151	Loss of serial communications for class 2 devices
U1152	Loss Of ACM Serial Data Communication
U1153	Loss Of CCP Communications
U1154 ... U1159	Loss of serial communications for class 2 devices
U1160	Loss Of DDM Communications
U1161	Loss Of Passenger's Door Module Simple Serial Data
U1162	Loss Of Rear Door Module Simple Bus Serial Data
U1163	Loss of serial communications for class 2 devices
U1164	Loss Of DIM Serial Data Communication

OBD II FAULT CODES

GM (Buick/Cadillac/Chevrolet/GMC/Oldsmobile/Pontiac/Saturn)

U1165	Loss of serial communications for class 2 devices
U1166	Loss Of MSM Communications
U1167	Loss of serial communications for class 2 devices
U1168	Loss Of TTM Communications
U1169	Loss Of MMM Communications
U1170	Loss Of Driver's Door Switch Assembly Simple Bus Serial Data
U1171 ... U1175	Loss of serial communications for class 2 devices
U1176	Loss Of RFA Communications
U1177 ... U1191	Loss of serial communications for class 2 devices
U1192	Loss Of VTD Communications
U1193	Loss of VIM Class 2 Communication
U1194 ... U1254	Loss of serial communications for class 2 devices
U1255	Generic Loss Of Communications
U1256 ... U1299	Loss of Class 2 serial data communications
U1300	Class 2 Shorted to Ground
U1301	Class 2 Shorted to Battery +
U1302	Loss of Class 2 serial data communications
U1303	Loss of Class 2 serial data communications
U1304	Loss Of UART Communications

GM (Buick/Cadillac/Chevrolet/GMC/Oldsmobile/Pontiac/Saturn)

U1305 ... U1999	Loss of Class 2 serial data communications

OBD II FAULT CODES

HONDA / ACURA

P1077	Intake Manifold Runner Control (IMRC) System Malfunction (Low RPM)
P1078	Intake Manifold Runner Control (IMRC) System Malfunction (High RPM)
P1106	Barometric Pressure Sensor Circuit
P1107	Barometric Pressure Sensor Circuit Low Voltage
P1108	Barometric Pressure Sensor Circuit High Voltage
P1121	Throttle Position (TP) Sensor Signal Lower Than Expected
P1122	Throttle Position (TP) Sensor Signal Higher Than Expected
P1128	Manifold Absolute Pressure (MAP) Sensor Signal Lower Than Expected
P1129	Manifold Absolute Pressure (MAP) Sensor Signal Higher Than Expected
P1162	HO2S-11 Circuit Fault (Bank 1 Sensor 1)
P1163	HO2S-11 Slow Response (Bank 1 Sensor 1)
P1164	HO2S-11 Circuit Fault (Bank 1 Sensor 1)
P1165	HO2S-11 Slow Response (Bank 1 Sensor 1)
P1166	HO2S-11 Heater Circuit Fault
P1167	HO2S-11 Heater Circuit (VS+) Fault
P1168	HO2S-11 Label Circuit Low Voltage Fault
P1169	HO2S-11 Label Circuit High Voltage Fault
P1201	Cylinder 1 Misfire Detected
P1202	Cylinder 2 Misfire Detected
P1203	Cylinder 3 Misfire Detected
P1204	Cylinder 4 Misfire Detected
P1205	Cylinder 5 Misfire Detected
P1206	Cylinder 6 Misfire Detected
P1241	Throttle Valve Control Motor Circuit '1' Fault
P1242	Throttle Valve Control Motor Circuit '2' Fault

HONDA / ACURA

P1243	Insufficient Throttle Position Detected
P1244	Insufficient Closed Throttle Position Detected
P1246	Accelerator Position Sensor '1' Circuit Fault
P1247	Accelerator Position Sensor '2' Cicuit Fault
P1248	Accelerator Pedal Position Sensor Correlation Fault
P1253	VTEC System Circuit Fault
P1259	VTEC System Circuit Fault (Bank 1)
P1279	VTEC System Circuit Fault (Bank 2)
P1297	Electrical Load Detector Circuit Low Voltage
P1298	Electrical Load Detector Circuit High Voltage
P1300	Random Misfire Detected
P1316	Spark Plug Detection Module Circuit Fault (Bank 2)
P1317	Spark Plug Detection Module Circuit Fault (Bank 1)
P1318	Spark Plug Detection Module Reset Fault (Bank 2)
P1319	Spark Plug Detection Module Reset Fault (Bank 1)
P1324	Knock Sensor Power Source Circuit Low Voltage
P1336	Crankshaft Speed Fluctuation Sensor Signal Fault
P1336	Crankshaft Speed Fluctuation Sensor 'B' Signal Fault
P1337	CKF Sensor Circuit Fault (No Signal)
P1337	Crankshaft Position Top Sensor 'B' Fault (No Signals)
P1359	Crankshaft Position Top Dead Center Sensor Fault
P1361	Top Dead Center Sensor Fault (Intermittent Signal)
P1362	Top Dead Center Sensor Fault (No Signal)
P1381	Camshaft Position Sensor Fault (Intermittent Signal)
P1382	Camshaft Position Sensor Fault (No Signal)

HONDA / ACURA

P1386	Camshaft Position Sensor 'B' Intermittent Signals
P1387	Camshaft Position Sensor 'B' No Signals
P1456	EVAP Control System leak Detected (Fuel Tank)
P1457	EVAP Control System leak Detected (Canister)
P1459	EGR Valve lift sensor insufficient flow detected
P1491	EGR Valve lift sensor insufficient lift
P1498	EGR Valve lift sensor high voltage
P1508 ... P1519	Idle Air control valve circuit fault
P1607	PCM (ECM) Internal Fault 'A'
P1608	PCM (ECM) Internal Fault 'B'
P1655	TMA or TMB signal line fault
P1671	TCM A/T FI Data line, no signal
P1672 ... P1677	TCM A/T FI Data line, failure detected
P1705	TCM A/T Gear position switch circuit shorted
P1706	TCM A/T Gear position switch circuit open
P1753	TCM A/T Lockup solenoid valve 'A' fault
P1758	TCM A/T Lockup solenoid valve 'B' fault
P1790	TCM A/T TP sensor circuit fault
P1791	TCM A/T vehicle speed sensor circuit fault
P1792	TCM A/T ECT sensor circuit fault

OBD II FAULT CODES

JAGUAR

P0065	Air Assisted Injector Control Range/Performance
P0066	Air Assisted Injector Control Circuit or Circuit Low
P1000	OBD Systems Readiness Test Not Complete
P1104	Mass Air Flow Sensor Circuit Ground
P1111	System Pass
P1121	Pedal Position Sensor A Circuit Range/Performance
P1122	Pedal Position Sensor A Circuit Low Input
P1123	Pedal Position Sensor A Circuit High Input
P1136	Control Box Fan Circuit
P1137	Lack Of HO2S12 Switches - Sensor Indicates Lean
P1138	Lack Of HO2S12 Switches - Sensor Indicates Rich
P1143	Air Assisted Injector Control Valve Range/Performance
P1144	Air Assisted Injector Control Valve Circuit
P1157	Lack Of HO2S22 Switches - Sensor Indicates Lean
P1158	Lack Of HO2S22 Switches - Sensor Indicates Rich
P1171	System Too Lean - Banks 1 and 2 (Lean Fuel Fault)
P1172	System Too Rich - Banks 1 and 2 (Rich Fuel Fault)
P1174	System Too Lean - Banks 1 and 2 (Suspect HO2S)
P1175	System Too Rich - Banks 1 and 2 (Suspect HO2S)
P1176	Long Term Fuel Trim Too Lean - Banks 1 and 2 (FMFR)
P1177	Long Term Fuel Trim Too Rich - Banks 1 and 2 (FMFR)
P1178	Long Term Fuel Trim Too Lean - Banks 1 and 2 (AMFR)
P1179	Long Term Fuel Trim Too Rich - Banks 1 and 2 (AMFR)
P1185	O2 Sensor Heater Circuit Open - Hardware Fault
P1186	O2 Sensor Heater Circuit Shorted - Hardware Fault

JAGUAR

P1187	O2 Sensor Heater Circuit Open - Inferred Fault
P1188	O2 Sensor Heater Circuit Resistance
P1189	O2 Sensor Heater Circuit Low Resistance Fault 1
P1190	O2 Sensor Heater Circuit Low Resistance Fault 2
P1191	O2 Sensor Heater Circuit Open - Hardware Fault
P1192	O2 Sensor Heater Circuit Shorted
P1193	O2 Sensor Heater Circuit Open - Inferred Fault
P1194	O2 Sensor Heater Circuit Resistance Fault
P1195	O2 Sensor Heater Circuit Low Resistance Fault 1
P1196	O2 Sensor Heater Circuit Low Resistance Fault 2
P1198	Fuel Level Input Circuit High
P1199	Fuel Level Input Circuit Low
P1201	Cylinder #1 Injector Circuit Open/Shorted
P1202	Cylinder #2 Injector Circuit Open/Shorted
P1203	Cylinder #3 Injector Circuit Open/Shorted
P1204	Cylinder #4 Injector Circuit Open/Shorted
P1205	Cylinder #5 Injector Circuit Open/Shorted
P1206	Cylinder #6 Injector Circuit Open/Shorted
P1207	Cylinder #7 Injector Circuit Open/Shorted
P1208	Cylinder #8 Injector Circuit Open/Shorted
P1221	Pedal Demand Sensor B Circuit Range/Performance
P1224	Electronic Throttle Control Position Error
P1226	Mechanical Guard Circuit Range/Performance
P1227	Mechanical Guard Circuit Low Input
P1228	Mechanical Guard Circuit High Input

JAGUAR

P1229	Electronic Throttle Control Circuit
P1230	Fuel Pump Relay
P1235	VSV 1/2/3 Circuit Range/Performance
P1236	VSV 1 Circuit
P1237	VSV 2 Circuit
P1238	VSV 3 Circuit
P1240	Sensor Power Supply
P1241	Sensor Power Supply Low Input
P1242	Sensor Power Supply High Input
P1243	Analog Ground
P1245	Crank Signal Low Input
P1246	Crank Signal High Input
P1250	Throttle Valve Spring
P1251	Throttle Position
P1252	VSV stuck on VA/VV
P1253	VSV Stuck on VR
P1260	Theft Detected, Vehicle Immobilized
P1313	Misfire Rate Catalyst Damage Fault - Bank 1
P1314	Misfire Rate Catalyst Damage Fault - Bank 2
P1315	Persistent Misfire
P1316	Misfire Rate Exceeds Emissions
P1336	Crankshaft/Camshaft Sensor Range/Performance
P1340	Camshaft Position Sensor B Circuit
P1341	Camshaft Position Sensor B Circuit Range/Performance
P1361	Ignition Coil, Cylinder #1, No Activation

JAGUAR

P1362	Ignition Coil, Cylinder #2, No Activation
P1363	Ignition Coil, Cylinder #3, No Activation
P1364	Ignition Coil, Cylinder #4, No Activation
P1365	Ignition Coil, Cylinder #5, No Activation
P1366	Ignition Coil, Cylinder #6, No Activation
P1367	Ignition System Failure Group 1
P1368	Ignition System Failure Group 2
P1370	Insufficient RPM Increase During Spark Test
P1371	Ignition Coil - Cylinder 1 - Early Activation Fault
P1372	Ignition Coil - Cylinder 2 - Early Activation Fault
P1373	Ignition Coil - Cylinder 3 - Early Activation Fault
P1374	Ignition Coil - Cylinder 4 - Early Activation Fault
P1375	Ignition Coil - Cylinder 5 - Early Activation Fault
P1376	Ignition Coil - Cylinder 6 - Early Activation Fault
P1384	Variable Valve Timing Solenoid A Circuit
P1392	Variable Valve Timing Solenoid A Circuit Low Input
P1393	Variable Valve Timing Solenoid A Circuit High Input
P1396	Variable Valve Timing Solenoid B Circuit
P1397	Variable Valve Timing Solenoid B Circuit Low Input
P1398	Variable Valve Timing Solenoid B Circuit High Input
P1400	Exhaust Gas Recirculation Valve Position Control
P1401	Exhaust Gas Recirculation Valve Position Circuit
P1408	Exhaust Gas Recirculation Thermister
P1409	Exhaust Gas Recirculation Valve Circuit
P1440	Purge Valve Stuck Open

JAGUAR

P1441	ELC System 1
P1447	ELC System Closure Valve Flow
P1448	ELC System 2
P1453	Fuel Tank Pressure Relief Valve Malfunction
P1454	Evaporative Emission Control System Vacuum Test
P1475	Fan Relay (Low) Circuit
P1476	Fan Relay (High) Circuit
P1508	Idle Air Control Circuit Open
P1509	Idle Air Control Circuit Shorted
P1514	High Load Neutral/Drive Fault
P1516	Gear Change Neutral/Drive Fault
P1517	Cranking Neutral/Drive Fault
P1534	Restraint Deployment Indicator Circuit
P1565	Speed Control Command Switch Out Of Range High
P1566	Speed Control Command Switch Out Of Range Low
P1567	Speed Control Output Circuit
P1568	Speed Control Unable to Hold Speed
P1571	Brake Switch
P1582	Electronic Throttle Monitor Data Available
P1600	Loss Of KAM Power, Circuit Open
P1603	EEPROM Malfunction
P1605	Keep Alive Memory Test Failure
P1606	ECM Control Relay Output Circuit
P1607	MIL Output Circuit
P1608	Watchdog Malfunction

JAGUAR

P1609	Internal Control Module CPU to CPU Communication Failure
P1611	Throttle Target Malfunction 1
P1612	Throttle Offset Malfunction
P1637	CAN Link ECM/ABS Control Module Circuit/Network
P1638	CAN Link ECM/INSTM Circuit/Network
P1641	Fuel Pump Primary Circuit
P1642	CAN Link Circuit
P1643	CAN Link Engine Control Module/Transmission Control Module Circuit/Network
P1646	Linear O2 Sensor Control Chip (Bank 1)
P1647	Linear O2 Sensor Control Chip (Bank 2)
P1648	Knock Sensor Input Chip
P1696	CAN Link Engine Control Module/Cruise Control Module Circuit/Network
P1697	Cruise Control Distance-Control Input Circuit
P1700	Transmission Indeterminate Failure (Failed to Neutral)
P1720	Vehicle Speed (Meter) Circuit
P1722	Stall Speed
P1726	Engine Overspeed
P1730	Gear Control Malfunction 2,3,5
P1731	Inconsistent Gear Ratio
P1734	Gear Control Malfunction
P1745	Pressure Regulator 1
P1746	Pressure Regulator 2
P1747	Pressure Regulator 3
P1748	Pressure Regulator 5
P1758	Presure Solenoid Control System Incorrect Current

JAGUAR

P1775	Transmission System MIL Fault
P1776	Ignition Retard Request Duration
P1777	Ignition Retard Request Circuit
P1778	Transmission Reverse I/P Circuit
P1779	Load Control
P1789 ... P1793	Ignition Supply Malfunction
P1794	Battery Voltage Circuit
P1795	Inconsistent CAN Level
P1796	CAN Controller Circuit (Bus off)
P1797	CAN TCM/ECM Circuit Malfunction
P1798	CAN TCM/INST Circuit Malfunction
P1799	CAN TCM/ABS Circuit Malfunction
P1882	Engine Coolant Level Switch Circuit Short To Ground

OBD II FAULT CODES

KIA

P1102	HO2S-11 heater circuit high voltage
P1105	HO2S-12 heater circuit high voltage
P1115	HO2S-11 heater circuit low voltage
P1117	HO2S-12 heater circuit low voltage
P1123	Long term trim adaptive air system low
P1124	Long term fuel trim adaptive air system high
P1127	Long term fuel trim multiplicative air system low
P1128	Long term fuel trim multiplicative air system high
P1140	Load calculation cross check
P1170	HO2S-11 circuit voltage stuck at Mid-range
P1195	EGR Boost or pressure sensor circuit fault
P1196	Ignition switch start circuit fault
P1213	Fuel injector 1 circuit high voltage
P1214	Fuel injector 2 circuit high voltage
P1215	Fuel injector 3 circuit high voltage
P1216	Fuel injector 4 circuit high voltage
P1225	Fuel injector 1 circuit low voltage
P1226	Fuel injector 2 circuit low voltage
P1227	Fuel injector 3 circuit low voltage
P1228	Fuel injector 4 circuit low voltage
P1250	Pressure regulator control solenoid circuit fault
P1345	No SGC (CMP) signal to PCM
P1386	Knock sensor control zero test
P1401	EGR control solenoid circuit signal low
P1402	EGR control solenoid circuit signal high

KIA

P1402	EGR valve position sensor circuit fault
P1410	EVAP purge control solenoid circuit high voltage
P1412	EGR differential pressure sensor signal low
P1413	EGR differential pressure sensor signal high
P1425	EVAP purge control solenoid circuit low voltage
P1449	Canister drain cut valve solenoid circuit fault
P1455	Fuel tank sending unit circuit fault
P1458	Air conditioning compressor clutch signal fault
P1485	EGR Vent control solenoid circuit fault
P1486	EGR vacuum control solenoid circuit fault
P1487	EGR boost sensor solenoid circuit fault
P1510	Idle air control valve closing coil high voltage
P1513	Idle air control valve closing coil low voltage
P1515	A/T to M/T codification
P1523	VICS solenoid valve circuit fault
P1552	Idle air control valve opening coil low voltage
P1553	Idle air control valve opening coil high voltage
P1606	Chassis accelerator sensor signal circuit fault
P1608	PCM internal fault
P1611	MIL request circuit low voltage
P1614	MIL request circuit high voltage
P1616	Chassis accelerator sensor signal low voltage
P1617	Chassis accelerator sensor signal high voltage
P1624	TCM to PCM MIL request signal circuit fault
P1655	Unused power stage 'B'

KIA

P1660	Power stage group 'B'
P1665	Power stage group 'A'
P1743	Torque converter clutch solenoid circuit fault
P1794	Battery or circuit fault
P1797	Clutch pedal switch (MT) -or- P/N switch circuit fault

OBD II FAULT CODES

LEXUS / TOYOTA

P1100	Barometric pressure sensor circuit fault
P1120	Accelerator Pedal Position Sensor Circuit Malfunction
P1121	Accelerator Pedal Position Sensor Range/Performance Problem
P1125	Throttle Control Motor Circuit Malfunction
P1128	Throttle Control Motor Lock Malfunction
P1129	Electric Throttle Control System Malfunction
P1130	Air-Fuel Sensor Circuit Range/Performance
P1133	Air-Fuel Sensor Circuit Response Malfunction
P1135	Air-Fuel Sensor Heater Circuit Response Malfunction
P1150	A/F Sensor Circuit Range/Performance Malfunction
P1153	A/F Sensor Circuit Response Malfunction
P1155	A/F Sensor Heater Circuit Malfunction
P1200	Fuel pump relay circuit fault
P1300	Igniter circuit fault (Bank 1)
P1305	Igniter circuit fault (Bank 2)
P1335	Crankshaft position sensor circuit fault
P1400	Sub-throttle position sensor circuit fault
P1401	Sub-throttle position sensor circuit fault
P1500	Starter signal circuit fault
P1510	Intake air volume too Low with supercharger ON
P1600	PCM Battery backup circuit fault
P1605	Knock control CPU fault
P1700	Vehicle speed sensor '2' circuit fault
P1705	Direct clutch speed circuit fault
P1765	Linear shift solenoid circuit fault
P1780	Park/Neutral position switch fault

OBD II FAULT CODES

MAZDA

P0010	A Camshaft Position Actuator Circuit (Bank 1)
P0011	A Camshaft Position Timing - Over-Advanced (Bank 1)
P0012	A Camshaft Position Timing - Over-Retarded (Bank 1)
P0031	HO2S Heater Control Circuit Low (bank 1, sensor 1)
P0032	HO2S Heater Control Circuit High (bank 1, sensor 1)
P0037	HO2S Heater Control Circuit Low (bank 1, sensor 2)
P0038	HO2S Heater Control Circuit High (bank 1, sensor 2)
P0043	HO2S Heater Control Circuit Low (bank 1, sensor 3)
P0044	HO2S Heater Control Circuit High (bank 1, sensor 3)
P0051	HO2S Heater Control Circuit Low (bank 2, sensor 1)
P0052	HO2S Heater Control Circuit High (bank 2, sensor 1)
P0057	HO2S Heater Control Circuit Low (bank 2, sensor 2)
P0058	HO2S Heater Control Circuit High (bank 2, sensor 2)
P1000	OBD Systems Readiness Test Not Complete
P1001	Activate self test SCP error
P1100	Mass Air Flow Sensor Circuit Intermittent
P1101	Mass Air Flow Sensor Out Of Self Test Range
P1102	Mass Air Flow Sensor In Range But Lower Than Expected
P1103	Mass Air Flow Sensor In Range But Higher Than Expected
P1110	Intake Air Temperature Circuit (dynamic chamber) Open/Short
P1112	Intake Air Temperature Circuit Intermittent
P1113	Intake Air Temperature Circuit (dynamic chamber) Open/Short
P1116	Engine Coolant Temperature Sensor Out Of Self Test Range
P1117	Engine Coolant Temperature Sensor Circuit Intermittent
P1120	TP sensor out of range low

OBD II FAULT CODES

MAZDA

P1121	TP sensor signal not consistent with MAF signal
P1122	Throttle Position Sensor A In Range But Lower Than Expected
P1123	Throttle Position Sensor A In Range But Higher Than Expected
P1124	TP sensor signal out of self test range
P1125	TP sensor signal intermittent
P1126	Throttle Position (Narrow Range) Sensor Circuit
P1127	HO2S-12 heater not ON during KOER self test
P1128	Upstream HO2S Sensors Swapped
P1129	Downstream HO2S Sensors Swapped
P1130	HO2S-11 not switching (fuel control limit reached)
P1131	HO2S-11 signal above 0.45v (A/F ratio too lean)
P1132	HO2S-11 signal below 0.45v (A/F ratio too rich)
P1133	Bank 1 Fuel Control Shifted Lean (FAOSC)
P1134	Bank 1 Fuel Control Shifted Rich (FAOSC)
P1135	HO2S11 Heater Circuit Low
P1136	HO2S11 Heater Circuit High
P1137	HO2S-11 signal above 0.45v (A/F ratio too rich)
P1138	Lack Of HO2S12 Switches - Sensor Indicates Rich
P1141	HO2S12 Heater Circuit Low
P1142	HO2S12 Heater Circuit High
P1143	Lack of HO2S Switches, HO2S13 Indicates Lean
P1144	Lack of HO2S Switches, HO2S13 Indicates Rich
P1150	HO2S-21 not switching (fuel control limit reached)
P1151	HO2S-21 signal below 0.45v (A/F ratio too rich)
P1152	HO2S-21 signal above 0.45v (A/F ratio too rich)

MAZDA

P1153	Bank 2 Fuel Control Shifted Lean (FAOSC)
P1154	Bank 2 Fuel Control Shifted Rich (FAOSC)
P1169	Feedback A/F Mixture Control (HO2S12)
P1170	HO2S-11 circuit too high or low (bank 1 sensor 1)
P1173	Feedback A/F Mixture Control (HO2S21)
P1182	Fuel Shut Off Solenoid Circuit
P1189	Pump Speed Signal
P1190	Calibration Resistor Out Of Range
P1191	TP (controlled) circuit
P1194	ECM/PCM A/D Converter
P1195	EGR boost sensor circuit fault
P1196	Ignition switch start circuit fault
P1197	Mileage Switch Circuit
P1213	Start Injector Circuit
P1221	Traction Control System
P1222	Traction Control Output Circuit
P1226	Control Sleeve Sensor Circuit
P1235	Fuel pump control out range
P1236	Fuel pump control out range
P1248	Turbo Boost Pressure Not Detected
P1250	Fuel Pressure Regulator Control Solenoid
P1251	Air Mixture Solenoid Circuit
P1252	Pressure regulator control solenoid '2' circuit fault
P1260	Anti-theft system signal detected, engine disabled
P1270	Engine RPM or vehicle speed limit reached

MAZDA

P1279	Control Sleeve Sensor Circuit Range/Performance
P1298	Injector Driver Module Failure
P1312	Injection Pump Timing Actuator Circuit
P1318	Injection Timing Piston Position Sensor Circuit
P1319	Injection Timing Piston Position Sensor Circuit Range/Performance
P1345	CMP or SGC sensor circuit fault
P1351	IDM signal lost to PCM or out of range
P1352	Ignition coil 'A' primary circuit fault
P1353	Ignition coil 'B' primary circuit fault
P1354	Ignition coil 'C' primary circuit fault
P1358	IDM signal out of self test range
P1359	SPOUT signal lost to PCM or out of range
P1360	Ignition coil 'A' secondary circuit fault
P1361	Ignition coil 'B' secondary circuit fault
P1362	Ignition coil 'C' secondary circuit fault
P1364	Ignition coil primary circuit fault
P1365	Ignition coil secondary circuit fault
P1382	Camshaft Position Timing Solenoid #1 Circuit
P1387	Camshaft Position Timing Solenoid #2 Circuit
P1390	Octane adjust shorting bar out or circuit open
P1400	DPFE sensor signal below self test minimum
P1401	DPFE sensor signal above self test maximum
P1402	EGR valve position sensor circuit fault
P1405	DPFE sensor upstream hose off or plugged
P1406	DPFE sensor downstream hose off or plugged

MAZDA

P1407	No EGR flow detected
P1408	EGR system flow out of KOER self test range
P1409	EGR vacuum regulator solenoid circuit fault
P1412	Exhaust Gas Recirculation Valve Frozen
P1415	Air Pump Circuit
P1416	Port Air Circuit
P1417	Port Air Relief Circuit
P1418	Split Air #1 Circuit
P1419	Split Air #2 Circuit
P1439	Floor Temp Switch Circuit
P1443	EVAP system purge flow fault
P1444	EVAP purge flow sensor circuit low voltage
P1445	EVAP purge flow sensor circuit high voltage
P1446	Evaporative Vacuum Solenoid Circuit
P1449	Evaporative Check Solenoid Circuit
P1450	Unable to Bleed Up Fuel Tank Vacuum
P1451	Evaporative Emission Control System Vent Control Circuit
P1455	Fuel tank level sensor circuit fault
P1456	Fuel Tank Temperature Sensor Circuit
P1457	Purge Solenoid Control System
P1460	Wide open throttle A/C cut-off relay circuit fault
P1464	Air conditioning control signal circuit fault
P1465	A/C Relay Circuit
P1473	Fan Circuit Open (VLCM)
P1474	Fan control system fault

MAZDA

P1475	Fan Relay (Low) Circuit
P1476	Fan Relay (High) Circuit
P1477	Additional Fan Relay Circuit
P1479	High Fan Control Primary Circuit
P1480	Fan Secondary Low With Low Fan On
P1481	Fan Secondary Low With High Fan On
P1485	EGR vacuum solenoid circuit fault
P1486	EGR vent solenoid circuit fault
P1487	Exhaust Gas Recirculation Check Solenoid Circuit
P1490	Secondary Air Relief Solenoid Circuit
P1491	Secondary Switch Solenoid Circuit
P1492	APLSOL Solenoid Circuit
P1493	RCNT Solenoid Circuit
P1494	SPCUT Solenoid Circuit
P1495	TCSPL Solenoid Circuit
P1496	EGR Stepper Motor 1 Control Circuit Low/High
P1497	EGR Stepper Motor 2 Control Circuit Low/High
P1498	EGR Stepper Motor 3 Control Circuit Low/High
P1499	EGR Stepper Motor 4 Control Circuit Low/High
P1500	Vehicle speed sensor intermittent signals
P1501	Vehicle speed sensor out of self test range
P1504	Idle air control solenoid circuit intermittent fault
P1505	Idle air control system at adaptive clip
P1506	IAC system overspeed detected during self test
P1507	IAC system underspeed detected during self test

MAZDA

P1508	Bypass air solenoid '1' circuit fault
P1509	Bypass air solenoid '2' circuit fault
P1510	Idle Signal Circuit
P1511	Idle Switch (Electric Control Throttle) Circuit
P1512	Intake Manifold Runner Control Stuck Closed (Bank 1)
P1515	Electric Current Circuit
P1521	Variable Resonance Induction System Solenoid #1 Circuit
P1522	Variable Resonance Induction System Solenoid #2 Circuit
P1523	VICS solenoid circuit fault
P1524	Variable Intake Solenoid Circuit
P1525	ABV vacuum solenoid circuit fault
P1526	ABV vent solenoid circuit fault
P1527	Bypass Air Solenoid (Accelerate Warmup) Circuit
P1528	Subsidiary Throttle Valve Solenoid Circuit
P1529	L/C atmospheric balance air control valve fault
P1540	Air Bypass Valve Circuit
P1562	PCM B+ Voltage Low (KAM power)
P1566	TCM B+ Voltage Low
P1569	Intake Manifold Runner Control Control Circuit Low
P1570	Intake Manifold Runner Control Control Circuit High
P1600	Loss Of KAM Power, Circuit Open
P1601	ECM/TCM Serial Communication Error
P1602	Immobilizer/ECM Communication Error
P1603	ID Number Unregistered
P1604	Code Word Unregistered

MAZDA

P1605	PCM keep active memory test error
P1608	PCM Internal Circuit
P1609	PCM (ECM CPU) knock sensor fault
P1621	Immobilizer Code Words Do Not Match
P1622	Immobilizer ID Does Not Match
P1623	Immobilizer Code Word/ID Number Write Failure
P1624	Anti-theft System
P1627	PCM (ECM/TCS) line communication error
P1628	PCM (ECM/TCS) ABV line communication error
P1630	Alternator Regulator #1 Control Circuit
P1631	Alternator Regulator #2 Control Circuit
P1633	Generator Control System - over charge
P1634	Generator Control System - no charge
P1645	Fuel Pump Resistor Switch Circuit
P1649	Fuel Injection Pump Module
P1650	Power steering pressure switch out of range fault
P1651	Power steering pressure switch circuit fault
P1652	Idle Air Control Monitor Disabled By PSPS Failed On
P1680 ... P1682	Metering Oil Pump Failure
P1683	Metering Oil Pump Temperature Sensor Circuit
P1684	Metering Oil Pump Position Sensor Circuit
P1685 ... P1688	Metering Oil Pump Stepping Motor Cont. Circuit

MAZDA

P1689	Oil Pressure Control Solenoid Circuit
P1690	Wastegate Solenoid Circuit
P1691	Turbo Pressure Control Solenoid Circuit
P1692	Turbo Control Solenoid Circuit
P1693	Turbo Charge Control Circuit
P1694	Turbo Charge Relief Circuit
P1701	A/T TR sensor reverse engagement error
P1703	Brake on/off switch out of self test range
P1705	Transmission Range Circuit Not Indicating Park/Neutral During Self Test
P1706	High Vehicle Speed Observed in Park
P1708	Clutch Switch Circuit
P1709	Clutch Pedal (or Park/Neutral Position) Switch Out Of Self Test Range
P1710	Transmission Control Module Solenoid/Internal Ground Circuit
P1711	A/T TFT sensor out of self test range
P1713	Transmission Fluid Temperature Sensor In Range Failure
P1719	Engine Torque Signal
P1720	Vehicle speed sensor '2' signal error
P1721	Gear 1 Incorrect Ratio
P1722	Gear 2 Incorrect Ratio
P1723	Gear 3 Incorrect Ratio
P1724	Gear 4 Incorrect Ratio
P1729	Transmission 4x4 low switch error during self test
P1735	First Gear Switch Circuit Failure
P1736	Second Gear Switch Circuit Failure
P1737	Lockup Solenoid

MAZDA

P1738	Shift Time Error
P1739	Slip Solenoid
P1741	Torque converter clutch control error
P1742	Torque converter clutch failed on, MIL is on
P1743	Torque converter clutch failed on, TCIL is on
P1744	Torque Converter Clutch Solenoid Circuit
P1745	Line Pressure Solenoid
P1746	Electronic pressure control solenoid circuit open
P1747	Electronic pressure control solenoid circuit short
P1748	Pressure Control Solenoid A
P1749	Electronic pressure control solenoid circuit low
P1751	Shift Solenoid A Circuit Open
P1752	Shift Solenoid A Circuit Short
P1754	Transmission coast clutch solenoid electrical fault
P1756	Shift Solenoid B Circuit Open
P1757	Shift Solenoid B Circuit Short
P1759	2-4 Brake Failsafe Valve Malfunction
P1761	Transmission shift solenoid '3' performance
P1763	Low and Reverse Brake Pressure Switch Circuit
P1764	Low and Reverse Brake Failsafe Valve Malfunction
P1765	Timing Solenoid Circuit
P1770	Clutch Solenoid Circuit
P1771	Throttle Position Sensor Circuit High Input
P1772	Throttle Position Sensor Circuit Low Input
P1775	Torque Down Signal #1 Circuit

MAZDA

P1776	Torque Down Signal #2 Circuit
P1777	Torque Down Response Signal Circuit
P1780	Transmission control switch electrical fault
P1781	Transmission 4x4 low switch out of range fault
P1783	Transmission fluid temperature too high
P1788	Pressure Control Solenoid B Open Circuit
P1789	Pressure Control Solenoid B Short Circuit
P1790	TP (Mechanical) Circuit
P1791	TP (Electric) Circuit
P1792	Barometer Pressure Circuit
P1793	Intake Air Volume Circuit
P1794	Battery Voltage Circuit
P1795	Idle Switch Circuit
P1796	Kick Down Switch Circuit
P1797	Clutch Pedal (or Park/Neutral) Position Switch Circuit
P1798	Coolant Temperature Circuit
P1799	Hold Switch Circuit

OBD II FAULT CODES

MERCEDES (diesel)

P1105	Atmospheric pressure sensor in control module
P1220	Fuel quantity actuator (Y23/1)
P1221	CAN communication, ETC or ETS interrupted
P1222	IFI accelerator pedal position sensor (R25/2)
P1223	Fuel rack position sensor (Y23/1/1)
P1335	CKP sensor (IFI)
P1350	Injection sensor solenoid
P1351	Injection sensor circuit
P1352	Needle Lift Sensor
P1401	EGR lifting sender (B28/3)
P1404	EGR control
P1465	EPW power
P1470	Pressure control flap vacuum transducer (Y31/2)
P1475	Resonance intake line switchover valve (Y22/7)
P1476	Resonance intake manifold switchover valve (Y22/6)
P1480	Preglow control
P1481	Glow plug failure
P1482	Preglow control module (N14/2)
P1520	Cruise control switch (S40)
P1610	Voltage supply missing -or- relay module (K40)
P1611	IFI Control module (N3/7)
P1612	IFI Control module (N3/7) voltage, circuit 15
P1613	IFI Control module (N3/7)
P1614	IFI Control module (N3/7) voltage -or- Fuel metering actuator (Y23/1k1) -or- Fuel rack position sensor (Y23/1/1)

MERCEDES (diesel)

P1615	IFI Control module (N3/7) supply voltage
P1617	Control module fault -or- Control module not coded
P1622	Electrohydraulic shut-off actutor (Y1/1)
P1625	Check Engine MIL
P1630	Drive authorization signal
P1705	Starter lock-out/backup lamp switch (S16/1)
P1780	Modulating pressure switchover valve (AT/CC)(Y3/4) -or- Upshift delay switchover valve (AT/CC)(Y3/5)
P1781	Upshift delay switchover valve (AT/CC)(Y3/5)

OBD II FAULT CODES

MERCEDES (gas)

P1146	Left hot film MGF sensor (B2/6)
P1147	Left ECT sensor (B11/9)
P1148	Left IAT sensor (B17/5)
P1149	Left Manifold pressure sensor (B28/1)
P1162	Left EA/CC/ISC actuator actual value potentiometer (M16/4r1, M16/4r2)
P1163	Oil level switch (S43)
P1176	Oil pressure sensor
P1177	Oil sensor, level-temperature implausible
P1179	Oil quality implausible
P1180	High oil temperature
P1181	Engine electric cooling fan, faulty
P1182	Start relay output stage, faulty
P1183	Output stage cylinder fadeout, valve 1
P1184	Output stage cylinder fadeout, valve 2
P1185	Water in oil
P1186	Safety fuel shutoff detected
P1225	Variable intake manifold switchover valve (Y22/6)
P1233	Throttle valve jamming
P1300	Left CKP sensor (L5/4)
P1355	Cylinder shut-off valve, right bank (Y80) does not close at cylinder cutoff
P1356	Cylinder shut-off valve, left bank (Y81) does not close at cylinder cutoff
P1357	Cylinder cutoff, inlet valve of a cylinder continuous to be operated at cylinder cutoff
P1358	Cylinder 5 exhaust valve is not operating at cylinder cutoff
P1359	Cylinder 2 exhaust valve is not operating at cylinder cutoff
P1360	Cylinder 3 exhaust valve is not operating at cylinder cutoff

MERCEDES (gas)

P1361	Cylinder 8 exhaust valve is not operating at cylinder cutoff
P1366	Exhaust flap switchover valve (Y93)
P1380	Inlet valve of a cylinder is not operated at cylinder cutoff
P1384	Left knock sensor 1 (A29g1)
P1385	Left knock sensor 2 (A29g2)
P1386	Knock sensor regulation from right ECM (N3/12) hardware failure
P1397	Left camshaft Hall-effect sensor (B6/2)
P1400	EGR switchover valve output stage (Y31-1)
P1420	AIR pump switchover valve (Y32)
P1437	Exhaust gas temperature sensor 1
P1443	Purge valve
P1444	Exhaust gas temperature sensor 2
P1453	AIR relay module (K17)
P1463	Left AIR system malfunction
P1490	Left purge control valve (Y58/2)
P1491	A/C refrigerant pressure too high
P1519	Right adjustable camshaft timing solenoid (Y49/2) (logic chain)
P1522	Left adjustable camshaft timing solenoid (Y49/1) (logic chain)
P1525	Right adjustable camshaft timing solenoid (Y49/2)
P1533	Left adjustable camshaft timing solenoid (Y49/1)
P1542	Pedal value sensor (B37)
P1550	AC compressor torque implausible
P1570	Start enable of DAS not sent
P1580	Throttle valve actuator (M16/6)
P1581	Left EA/CC/ISC actuator (M16/4)

MERCEDES (gas)

P1584	Stop lamp switch (S9/1)
P1587	Left ECM (N3/11) voltage supply
P1588	CAN signal from RCL control module (N54) to left ECM (N3/11) interrupted
P1589	Knock sensor regulation from left ECM (N3/11) hardware failure
P1603	No or incorrect CAN message from control unit EIS
P1605	Rough road detected by signal from comparing wheel speeds
P1632	Left engine control module (N3/11)
P1642	ECU incorrectly coded
P1643	ECU incorrectly coded -or- CAN from transmission
P1644	Transmission version can't be checked due to low voltage at transmission ECU
P1681	Crash Sensor, signal implausible or frontal crash or short to power
P1747	CAN signal from ETC (N15/3) interrupted

OBD II FAULT CODES

MITSUBISHI

P1100	Induction control motor position sensor fault
P1101	Traction control vacuum solenoid circuit fault
P1102	Traction control ventilation solenoid circuit fault
P1103	Turbocharger waste gate actuator circuit fault
P1104	Turbocharger waster Gate solenoid circuit fault
P1105	Fuel pressure solenoid circuit fault
P1294	Target Idle speed not reached
P1295	No 5-volt supply to TP sensor
P1296	No 5-volt supply to MAP sensor
P1297	No charge in MAP from start to run
P1300	Ignition timing adjustment circuit fault
P1390	Timing belt skipped one tooth or more
P1391	Intermittent loss of CMP or CKP sensor signals
P1400	Manifold differential pressure sensor fault
P1443	EVAP purge control solenoid '2' circuit fault
P1486	EVAP leak monitor pinched hose detected
P1487	High speed radiator fan control relay circuit fault
P1489	High speed condenser fan control relay fault
P1490	Low speed fan control relay fault
P1492	Battery temperature sensor high voltage
P1494	EVAP ventilation switch or mechanical fault
P1495	EVAP ventilation solenoid circuit fault
P1496	5 Volt supply output too low
P1500	Generator FR terminal circuit fault
P1600	PCM/TCM serial communication link circuit fault

MITSUBISHI

P1696	PCM failure- EEPROM write denied
P1698	NO CCD messages from TCM
P1715	TCM pulse generator circuit fault
P1750	Pressure control, shift control, TCC solenoid fault
P1791	PCM ECT level signal to TCM circuit fault
P1899	P/N position/transaxle range switch circuit fault

OBD II FAULT CODES

NISSAN / INFINITI

P1105	MAP/BARO Pressure Switch Solenoid Valve
P1110	Intake Valve Timing Control Solenoid
P1120	Secondary throttle position sensor circuit fault
P1125	Tandem throttle position sensor circuit fault
P1130	Swirl Control Valve Control Solenoid Valve
P1135	Intake Valve Timing Control Circuit (Bank 2)
P1140	Intake Valve Timing Control Position Sensor (Bank 1)
P1145	Intake Valve Timing Control Position Sensor (Bank 2)
P1148	Closed Loop
P1165	Swirl Control Valve Control Vacuum Switch
P1168	Closed Loop Fault Detected (Bank 2)
P1210	Traction control system signal fault
P1220	Fuel pump control signal fault
P1320	Ignition control signal fault
P1336	Crankshaft position sensor circuit fault
P1400	EGR/EVAP control solenoid circuit fault
P1401	EGR temperature sensor circuit fault
P1402	EGR System
P1440	EVAP System Small Leak
P1441	Vacuum Cut Valve Bypass Valve
P1443	EVAP canister control vacuum switch circuit fault
P1605	TCM A/T diagnosis communication line fault
P1701	Fuel Trim
P1705	Throttle position sensor (switch) circuit fault
P1760	Overrun clutch solenoid valve circuit fault

OBD II FAULT CODES

SUBARU

P0031	Front oxygen (A/F) sensor heater circuit low input
P0032	Front oxygen (A/F) sensor heater circuit high input
P0037	Rear oxygen sensor heater circuit malfunction
P0038	Rear oxygen sensor heater circuit high input
P0065	Air assist injector solenoid valve malfunction
P0066	Air assist injector solenoid valve circuit low input
P0067	Air assist injector solenoid valve circuit high input
P1086	Tumble generator valve #2 (LH) position sensor circuit low input
P1087	Tumble generator valve #2 (LH) position sensor circuit high input
P1088	Tumble generator valve #1 (RH) position sensor circuit low input
P1089	Tumble generator valve #1 (RH) position sensor circuit high input
P1090	Tumble generator valve #1 (RH) malfunction (stuck open)
P1091	Tumble generator valve #1 (RH) malfunction (stuck close)
P1092	Tumble generator valve #2 (LH) malfunction (stuck open)
P1093	Tumble generator valve #2 (LH) malfunction (stuck close)
P1094	Tumble generator valve circuit #1 (open circuit)
P1095	Tumble generator valve circuit #1 (over-current)
P1096	Tumble generator valve circuit #2 (open circuit)
P1097	Tumble generator valve circuit #2 (over-current)
P1100	Starter switch circuit fault
P1101	Neutral position switch circuit fault (MT)
P1101	Neutral position (inhibitor) switch circuit fault (AT)
P1102	Pressure sources switching solenoid circuit fault
P1103	Engine torque control signal circuit fault
P1104	Traction control system signal circuit fault

OBD II FAULT CODES

SUBARU

P1107	AIR system diagnosis solenoid circuit fault
P1110	Atmospheric pressure sensor low input
P1111	Atmospheric pressure sensor high input
P1112	Atmospheric pressure sensor range/performance problem
P1130	Front oxygen sensor circuit malfunction (open circuit)
P1131	Front oxygen sensor circuit malfunction (short circuit)
P1134	Front oxygen (A/F) sensor microcomputer problem
P1137	Front oxygen (A/F) sensor circuit range/performance problem
P1139	Front oxygen (A/F) sensor #1 heater circuit performance/range problem
P1141	Mass air flow sensor circuit range/performance problem (low input)
P1142	Throttle position sensor circuit range/performance problem (low input)
P1146	Pressure sensor circuit range/performance problem (high input)
P1230	Fuel pump control unit malfunction
P1244	Wastegate control solenoid valve malfunction (low input)
P1245	Wastegate control solenoid valve malfunction (fail-safe)
P1301	Fire due to increased exhaust temperature
P1312	Exhaust temperature sensor malfunction
P1400	Fuel tank pressure control solenoid valve circuit low input
P1401	Fuel tank pressure control system performance
P1402	Fuel level pressure sensor circuit fault
P1420	Fuel tank pressure control solenoid valve circuit high input
P1443	Evaporative emission control system vent control function problem
P1480	Cooling fan relay 1 circuit high input
P1500	Cooling sub fan relay '1' circuit fault
P1502	Radiator fan performance

SUBARU

P1507	Idle control system malfunction (fail-safe)
P1510	Idle air control solenoid valve signal 1 circuit low input
P1511	Idle air control solenoid valve signal 1 circuit high input
P1512	Idle air control solenoid valve signal 2 circuit low input
P1513	Idle air control solenoid valve signal 2 circuit high input
P1514	Idle air control solenoid valve signal 3 circuit low input
P1515	Idle air control solenoid valve signal 3 circuit high input
P1516	Idle air control solenoid valve signal 4 circuit low input
P1517	Idle air control solenoid valve signal 4 circuit high input
P1518	Starter switch circuit low input
P1540	Vehicle speed sensor malfunction 2
P1544	High exhaust temperature detected
P1560	Back-up voltage circuit malfunction
P1590	Neutral position switch circuit high input
P1591	Neutral position switch circuit low input
P1592	Neutral position switch circuit (MT model)
P1594	Automatic transmission diagnosis input signal circuit malfunction
P1595	Automatic transmission diagnosis input signal circuit low input
P1596	Automatic transmission diagnosis input signal circuit high input
P1698	Engine torque control cut signal circuit low input
P1699	Engine torque control cut signal circuit high input
P1700	Cruise control system set signal circuit fault
P1701	Cruise control set signal circuit malfunction for automatic transmission
P1702	TCM diagnosis input signal circuit fault
P1703	Low clutch timing control solenoid valve circuit malfunction

SUBARU

P1711	Engine torque control signal 1 circuit malfunction
P1712	Engine torque control signal 2 circuit malfunction

OBD II FAULT CODES

SUZUKI

P1250	EFE Heater circuit fault
P1408	Manifold differential pressure sensor circuit fault
P1410	Fuel tank pressure control solenoid circuit fault
P1450	Barometric pressure sensor too low or too high
P1451	Barometric pressure sensor performance
P1460	Radiator fan control system fault
P1500	Engine starter signal circuit fault
P1510	PCM backup power supply circuit fault
P1530	Ignition timing adjustment switch circuit fault
P1600	PCM/TCM serial communication circuit fault
P1700	TCM throttle position sensor circuit fault
P1705	TCM ECT sensor circuit fault
P1710	Back-Up Signal For Speed Sensor Circuit Malfunction
P1715	PNP switch circuit fault
P1717	AT Drive range signal circuit fault
P1875	4WD Low Switch Circuit Malfunction
P1895	TCM To ECM Torque Reduction Circuit Malfunction

OBD II FAULT CODES

VW / AUDI / SKODA / SEAT

P1101	O2 Sensor Circuit, Bank1-Sensor1, Voltage too Low/Air Leak
P1102	O2 Sensor Heating Circuit, Bank1-Sensor1, Short to B+
P1103	O2 Sensor Heating Circuit, Bank1-Sensor1, Output too Low
P1104	Bank1-Sensor2, Voltage too Low/Air Leak
P1105	O2 Sensor Heating Circuit, Bank1-Sensor2, Short to B+
P1106	O2 Sensor Circuit, Bank2-Sensor1, Voltage too Low/Air Leak
P1107	O2 Sensor Heating Circuit, Bank2-Sensor1, Short to B+
P1108	O2 Sensor Heating Circuit, Bank2-Sensor1, Output too Low
P1109	O2 Sensor Circuit, Bank2-Sensor2, Voltage too Low/Air Leak
P1110	O2 Sensor Heating Circuit, Bank2-Sensor2, Short to B+
P1111	O2 Control (Bank 1), System too Lean
P1112	O2 Control (Bank 1), System too rich
P1113	Bank1-Sensor1, resistant too high
P1114	Bank1-Sensor2, resistant too high
P1115	O2 Sensor Heater Circuit, Bank1-Sensor1, Short to Ground
P1116	O2 Sensor Heater Circuit, Bank1-Sensor1, Open
P1117	O2 Sensor Heater Circuit, Bank1-Sensor2, Short to Ground
P1118	O2 Sensor Heater Circuit, Bank1-Sensor2, Open
P1119	O2 Sensor Heater Circuit, Bank2-Sensor1, Short to Ground
P1120	O2 Sensor Heater Circuit, Bank2-Sensor1, Open
P1121	O2 Sensor Heater Circuit, Bank2-Sensor2, Short to Ground
P1122	O2 Sensor Heater Circuit, Bank2-Sensor2, Open
P1123	Long Term Fuel Trim Add. Air., Bank1, System too Rich
P1124	Long Term Fuel Trim Add. Air., Bank1, System too Lean
P1125	Long Term Fuel Trim Add. Air., Bank2, System too Rich

VW / AUDI / SKODA / SEAT

P1126	Long Term Fuel Trim Add. Air., Bank2, System too Lean
P1127	Long Term Fuel Trim mult., Bank1, System too Rich
P1128	Long Term Fuel Trim mult., Bank1, System too Lean
P1129	Long Term Fuel Trim mult., Bank2, System too Rich
P1130	Long Term Fuel Trim mult., Bank2, System too Lean
P1131	Bank2-Sensor1, resistant too high
P1132	O2 Sensor Heating Circuit, Bank1+2-Sensor1, Short to B+
P1133	O2 Sensor Heating Circuit, Bank1+2-Sensor1, Electrical Malfunction
P1134	O2 Sensor Heating Circuit, Bank1+2-Sensor2, Short to B+
P1135	O2 Sensor Heating Circuit, Bank1+2-Sensor2, Electrical Malfunction
P1136	Long Term Fuel Trim Add. Fuel, Bank1, System too Lean
P1137	Long Term Fuel Trim Add. Fuel, Bank1, System too Rich
P1138	Long Term Fuel Trim Add. Fuel, Bank2, System too Lean
P1139	Long Term Fuel Trim Add. Fuel, Bank2, System too Rich
P1140	Bank2-Sensor2, resistant too high
P1141	Load Calculation Cross Check, Range/Performance
P1142	Load Calculation Cross Check, Lower Limit Exceeded
P1143	Load Calculation Cross Check, Upper Limit Exceeded
P1144	Mass or Volume Air Flow Circuit, Open/Short to Ground
P1145	Mass or Volume Air Flow Circuit, Short to B+
P1146	Mass or Volume Air Flow Circuit, Power Supply Malfunction
P1147	O2 Control (Bank 2), System too Lean
P1148	O2 Control (Bank 2), System too rich
P1149	O2 Control (Bank 1), out of range.
P1150	O2 Control (Bank 2), out of range

VW / AUDI / SKODA / SEAT

P1151	Bank1, Long Term Fuel Trim, Range 1, Leanness Lower Limit Exceeded
P1152	Bank1, Long Term Fuel Trim, Range 2, Leanness Lower Limit Exceeded
P1154	Manifold Switch Over, Malfunction
P1155	Manifold Absolute Pressure Sensor Circuit, Short to B+
P1156	Manifold Absolute Pressure Sensor Circuit, Open/Short to Ground
P1157	Manifold Absolute Pressure Sensor Circuit, Power Supply Malfunction
P1158	Manifold Absolute Pressure Sensor Circuit, Range/Performance
P1160	Manifold Temperature Sensor Circuit, Short to Ground
P1161	Manifold Temperature Sensor Circuit, Open/Short to B+
P1162	Fuel Temperature Sensor Circuit, Short to Ground
P1163	Fuel Temperature Sensor Circuit, Open/Short to B+
P1164	Fuel temperature sensor, range/Performance
P1165	Bank1, Long Term Fuel Trim, Range 1, Leanness Lower Limit Exceeded
P1166	Bank1, Long Term Fuel Trim, Range 2, Fatness Upper Limit Exceeded
P1171	Throttle Actuation Potentiometer Signal 2, Range/Performance
P1172	Throttle Actuation Potentiometer Signal 2, Signal too Low
P1173	Throttle Actuation Potentiometer Signal 2, Signal too High
P1174	Fuel Trim, Bank 1, different injection times
P1176	O2 Correction Behind Catalyst, B1, Limit Attained
P1177	O2 Correction Behind Catalyst, B2, Limit Attained
P1178	Linear Lambda probe / pump current, Open
P1179	Linear Lambda probe / pump current, short to Ground
P1180	Linear Lambda probe / pump current, short to B+
P1181	Linear Lambda probe / reference voltage, Open
P1182	Linear Lambda probe / reference voltage, short to Ground

VW / AUDI / SKODA / SEAT

P1183	Linear Lambda probe / reference voltage, short to B+
P1184	Linear Lambda probe / common ground wire, Open
P1185	Linear Lambda probe / common ground wire, short to Ground
P1186	Linear Lambda probe / common ground wire, short to B+
P1187	Linear Lambda probe/compensation resistor, Open
P1188	Linear Lambda probe/compensation resistor, short to Ground
P1189	Linear Lambda probe/compensation resistor, short to B+
P1190	Linear O2 Sensor / Reference Voltage, Incorrect Signal
P1196	O2 Sensor Heater Circuit, Bank1-Sensor1, Electrical Malfunction
P1197	O2 Sensor Heater Circuit, Bank2-Sensor1, Electrical Malfunction
P1198	O2 Sensor Heater Circuit, Bank1-Sensor2, Electrical Malfunction
P1199	O2 Sensor Heater Circuit, Bank2-Sensor2, Electrical Malfunction
P1201	Cylinder 1-Fuel Injector Circuit, Electrical Malfunction
P1202	Cylinder 2-Fuel Injector Circuit, Electrical Malfunction
P1203	Cylinder 3-Fuel Injector Circuit, Electrical Malfunction
P1204	Cylinder 4-Fuel Injector Circuit, Electrical Malfunction
P1205	Cylinder 5-Fuel Injector Circuit, Electrical Malfunction
P1206	Cylinder 6-Fuel Injector Circuit, Electrical Malfunction
P1207	Cylinder 7-Fuel Injector Circuit, Electrical Malfunction
P1208	Cylinder 8-Fuel Injector Circuit, Electrical Malfunction
P1209	Intake valves for cylinder shut-off, Short circuit to Ground
P1210	Intake valves for cylinder shut-off, Short to B+
P1211	Intake valves for cylinder shut-off, Open circuit.
P1213	Cylinder 1-Fuel Injector Circuit, Short to B+
P1214	Cylinder 2-Fuel Injector Circuit, Short to B+

VW / AUDI / SKODA / SEAT

P1215	Cylinder 3-Fuel Injector Circuit, Short to B+
P1216	Cylinder 4-Fuel Injector Circuit, Short to B+
P1217	Cylinder 5-Fuel Injector Circuit, Short to B+
P1218	Cylinder 6-Fuel Injector Circuit, Short to B+
P1219	Cylinder 7-Fuel Injector Circuit, Short to B+
P1220	Cylinder 8-Fuel Injector Circuit, Short to B+
P1225	Cylinder 1-Injector Circuit, Short to Ground
P1226	Cylinder 2-Injector Circuit, Short to Ground
P1227	Cylinder 3-Injector Circuit, Short to Ground
P1228	Cylinder 4-Injector Circuit, Short to Ground
P1229	Cylinder 5-Injector Circuit, Short to Ground
P1230	Cylinder 6-Injector Circuit, Short to Ground
P1231	Cylinder 7-Injector Circuit, Short to Ground
P1232	Cylinder 8-Injector Circuit, Short to Ground
P1237	Cylinder 1-Injector Circuit, Open Circuit
P1238	Cylinder 2-Injector Circuit, Open Circuit
P1239	Cylinder 3-Injector Circuit, Open Circuit
P1240	Cylinder 4-Injector Circuit, Open Circuit
P1241	Cylinder 5-Injector Circuit, Open Circuit
P1242	Cylinder 6-Injector Circuit, Open Circuit
P1243	Cylinder 7-Injector Circuit, Open Circuit
P1244	Cylinder 8-Injector Circuit, Open Circuit
P1245	Needle Lift Sensor Circuit, Short to Ground
P1246	Needle Lift Sensor Circuit, Range/Performance
P1247	Needle Lift Sensor Circuit, Open/Short to B+

OBD II FAULT CODES

VW / AUDI / SKODA / SEAT

P1248	Injection Start Control, Deviation
P1249	Fuel consumption signal, Electrical Fault in Circuit
P1250	Fuel Level, Too Low
P1251	Start of Injection Solenoid Circuit, Short to B+
P1252	Start of Injection Solenoid Circuit, Open/Short to Ground
P1253	Fuel consumption signal, short to Ground
P1254	Fuel consumption signal, short to B+
P1255	Engine Coolant Temperature Circuit, Short to Ground
P1256	Engine Coolant Temperature Circuit, Open/Short to B+
P1257	Engine Coolant System Valve, Open
P1258	Engine Coolant System Valve, Short to B+
P1259	Engine Coolant System Valve, Short to Ground
P1280	Fuel Injection Air Control Valve Circuit, Flow too low
P1283	Fuel Injection Air Control Valve Circuit, Electrical Malfunction
P1284	Fuel Injection Air Control Valve Circuit, Open
P1285	Fuel Injection Air Control Valve Circuit, Short to Ground
P1286	Fuel Injection Air Control Valve Circuit, Short to B+
P1287	Turbocharger bypass valve, Open
P1288	Turbocharger bypass valve, short to B+
P1289	Turbocharger bypass valve, short to Ground
P1300	Misfire detected, Reason: Fuel level too Low
P1319	Knock Sensor 1 Circuit, Short to Ground
P1320	Knock Sensor 2 Circuit, Short to Ground
P1321	Knock Sensor 3 Circuit, Low Input
P1322	Knock Sensor 3 Circuit, High Input

VW / AUDI / SKODA / SEAT

P1323	Knock Sensor 4 Circuit, Low Input
P1324	Knock Sensor 4 Circuit, High Input
P1325	Cylinder 1-Knock Control, Limit Attained
P1326	Cylinder 2-Knock Control, Limit Attained
P1327	Cylinder 3-Knock Control, Limit Attained
P1328	Cylinder 4-Knock Control, Limit Attained
P1329	Cylinder 5-Knock Control, Limit Attained
P1330	Cylinder 6-Knock Control, Limit Attained
P1331	Cylinder 7-Knock Control, Limit Attained
P1332	Cylinder 8-Knock Control, Limit Attained
P1335	Engine Torque Monitoring 2, Control Limit Exceeded
P1336	Engine torque control, Adaptation at Limit
P1337	Camshaft Position Sensor, Bank1, Short to Ground
P1338	Camshaft Position Sensor, Bank1, Open Circuit /Short to B+
P1339	Crankshaft Position /Engine Speed Sensor, Cross Connected
P1340	Camshaft/ Crankshaft Position Sensor Signals, Out of Sequence
P1341	Ignition Coil Power Output Stage 1, Short to Ground
P1342	Ignition Coil Power Output Stage 1, Short to B+
P1343	Ignition Coil Power Output Stage 2, Short to Ground
P1344	Ignition Coil Power Output Stage 2, Short to B+
P1345	Ignition Coil Power Output Stage 3, Short to Ground
P1346	Ignition Coil Power Output Stage 3, Short to B+
P1347	Bank2, Crankshaft-/Camshaft Position Sensor Signal, Out of Sequence
P1348	Ignition Coil Power Output Stage 1, Open
P1349	Ignition Coil Power Output Stage 2, Open

VW / AUDI / SKODA / SEAT

P1350	Ignition Coil Power Output Stage 3, Open
P1354	Modulation Piston Displ. Sensor Circuit, Malfunction
P1355	Cylinder 1, ignition circuit, Open
P1356	Cylinder 1, ignition circuit, short to B+
P1357	Cylinder 1, ignition circuit, short to Ground
P1358	Cylinder 2, ignition circuit, Open
P1359	Cylinder 2, ignition circuit, short to B+
P1360	Cylinder 2, ignition circuit, short to Ground
P1361	Cylinder 3, ignition circuit, Open
P1362	Cylinder 3, ignition circuit, short to B+
P1363	Cylinder 3, ignition circuit, short to Ground
P1364	Cylinder 4 ignition circuit, Open
P1365	Cylinder 4 ignition circuit, short to B+
P1366	Cylinder 4 ignition circuit, short to Ground
P1367	Cylinder 5, ignition circuit, Open
P1368	Cylinder 5, ignition circuit, short to B+
P1369	Cylinder 5, ignition circuit, short to Ground
P1370	Cylinder 6, ignition circuit, open
P1371	Cylinder 6, ignition circuit, short to B+
P1372	Cylinder 6, ignition circuit, short to Ground
P1373	Cylinder 7, ignition circuit, Open
P1374	Cylinder 7, ignition circuit, short to B+
P1375	Cylinder 7, ignition circuit, short to Ground
P1376	Cylinder 8, ignition circuit, Open
P1377	Cylinder 8, ignition circuit, short to B+

VW / AUDI / SKODA / SEAT

P1378	Cylinder 8, ignition circuit, short to Ground
P1386	Internal Control Module, Knock Control Circuit Error.
P1387	Control unit, internal altitude sensor
P1388	Control unit, internal throttle control
P1391	Camshaft Position Sensor, Bank2, Short to Ground
P1392	Camshaft Position Sensor, Bank2, Open Circuit /Short to B+
P1393	Ignition Coil Power Output Stage 1, Electrical Malfuntion
P1394	Ignition Coil Power Output Stage 2, Electrical Malfuntion
P1395	Ignition Coil Power Output Stage 3, Electrical Malfuntion
P1396	Engine Speed Sensor, Missing Tooth
P1397	Engine speed wheel, Adaptation at Limit
P1398	Engine RPM signal, short to ground
P1399	Engine RPM signal, short to B+
P1400	EGR Valve Circuit, Electrical Malfuntion
P1401	EGR Valve Circuit, Short to Ground
P1402	EGR Valve Circuit, Short to B+
P1403	EGR Flow, Deviation
P1404	EGR Flow, Adaptation not carried out
P1406	EGR Temperature Sensor, Range/Performance
P1407	EGR Temperature Sensor, Signal too Low
P1408	EGR Temperature Sensor, Signal too High
P1409	Tank Ventilation Valve, Electrical Malfunction
P1410	Tank Ventilation Valve, Short to B+
P1411	Secondary Air Injection System, Bank2, Flow too Low
P1412	EGR Differential Pressure Sensor, Signal too Low

VW / AUDI / SKODA / SEAT

P1413	EGR Differential Pressure Sensor, Signal too High
P1414	Secondary Air Injection System, Bank2, Leak Detected
P1417	Fuel Level Sensor, Signal too Low
P1418	Fuel Level Sensor, Signal too High
P1420	Secondary Air Injection Valve Circuit, Electrical Malfunction
P1421	Secondary Air Injection Valve Circuit, Short to Ground
P1422	Secondary Air Injection System Control Valve Circuit, Short to B+
P1423	Secondary Air Injection System, Bank1, Flow too Low
P1424	Secondary Air Injection System, Bank1, Leak Detected
P1425	Tank Ventilation Valve, Short to Ground
P1426	Tank Ventilation Valve, Open
P1432	Secondary Air Injection Valve, Open
P1433	Secondary Air Injection System Pump Relay Circ, Open
P1434	Secondary Air Injection System Pump Relay Circuit, Short to B+
P1435	Secondary Air Injection System Pump Relay Circ, Short to Ground
P1436	Secondary Air Injection System Pump Relay Circuit, Electrical Malfunction
P1439	EGR Valve Position Sensor, Adaptation at Limit
P1440	EGR Valve Power Stage, Open
P1441	EGR Valve Circuit, Open/Short to Ground
P1442	EGR Valve Position Sensor, Signal too high
P1443	EGR Valve Position Sensor, Signal too Low
P1444	EGR Valve Position Sensor, range/Performance
P1445	Catalyst Temperature Sensor 2 Circuit, Range/Performance
P1446	Catalyst Temperature Circuit, Short to Ground
P1447	Catalyst Temperature Circuit, Open/Short to B+

VW / AUDI / SKODA / SEAT

P1448	Catalyst Temperature Sensor 2 Circuit, Short to Ground
P1449	Catalyst Temperature Sensor 2 Circuit, Open/Short to B+
P1450	Secondary Air Injection System Circuit
P1451	Secondary Air Injection System Circuit, Short to Ground
P1452	Secondary Air Injection System, Open Circuit
P1453	Exhaust gas temperature sensor 1, open/short to B+
P1454	Exhaust gas temperature sensor 1, short to ground
P1455	Exhaust gas temperature sensor 1, range/performance
P1456	Exhaust gas temperature control bank 1, limit attained
P1457	Exhaust gas temperature sensor 2, open/short to B+
P1458	Exhaust gas temperature sensor 2, short to ground
P1459	Exhaust gas temperature sensor 2, range/performance
P1460	Exhaust gas temperature control bank 2, limit attained
P1461	Exhaust gas temperature control bank 1, range/performance
P1462	Exhaust gas temperature control bank 2, range/performance
P1465	Additive Pump, Short to B+
P1466	Additive Pump, Open/Short to Ground
P1467	EVAP Canister Purge Solenoid Valve, Short to B+
P1468	EVAP Canister Purge Solenoid Valve, Short to Ground
P1469	EVAP Canister Purge Solenoid Valve, Open
P1470	EVAP Emission Control System LDP Circuit, Electrical Malfunction
P1471	EVAP Emission Control System LDP Circuit, Short to B+
P1472	EVAP Emission Control System LDP Circuit, Short to Ground
P1473	EVAP Emission Control System LDP, Open Circuit
P1474	EVAP Canister Purge Solenoid Valve, electrical malfunction

VW / AUDI / SKODA / SEAT

P1475	EVAP Emission Control LDP Circuit, Malfunction/Signal Circuit Open
P1476	EVAP Emission Control LDP Circuit, Malfunction/Insufficient Vacuum
P1477	EVAP Emission Control LDP Circuit, Malfunction
P1478	EVAP Emission Control LDP Circuit, Clamped Tube Detected
P1500	Fuel Pump Relay Circuit, Electrical Malfunction
P1501	Fuel Pump Relay Circuit, Short to Ground
P1502	Fuel Pump Relay Circuit, Short to B+
P1503	Load signal from generator, range/Performance
P1504	Intake Air System Bypass, Leak Detected
P1505	Closed Throttle Position, Does Not Close/Open Circuit
P1506	Closed Throttle Position Switch, Does Not Open/Short to Ground
P1507	Idle System Learned Value, Lower Limit Attained
P1508	Idle System Learned Value, Upper Limit Attained
P1509	Idle Air Control Circuit, Electrical Malfunction
P1510	Idle Air Control Circuit, Short to B+
P1511	Intake Manifold Changeover Valve Circuit, Electrical Malfunction
P1512	Intake Manifold Changeover Valve circuit, Short to B+
P1512	Intake Manifold Changeover Valve Circuit, Short to B+
P1513	Intake Manifold Changeover Valve2 circuit, Short to B+
P1514	Intake Manifold Changeover Valve2 circuit, Short to Ground
P1515	Intake Manifold Changeover Valve, Short to Ground
P1516	Intake Manifold Changeover Valve, Open
P1517	Main Relay Circuit, Electrical Malfunction
P1518	Main Relay Circuit, Short to B+
P1519	Intake Camshaft Control, Bank1, Malfunction

VW / AUDI / SKODA / SEAT

P1520	Intake Manifold Changeover Valve2 circuit, Open
P1521	Intake Manifold Changeover Valve2 circuit, electrical Malfunction
P1522	Intake Camshaft Control, Bank2, Malfunction
P1523	Crash Signal from Airbag Control Unit, range/performance
P1525	Intake Camshaft Control Circuit, Bank1, Electrical Malfunction
P1526	Intake Camshaft Control Circuit, Bank1, Short to B+
P1527	Intake Camshaft Control Circuit, Bank1, Short to Ground
P1528	Intake Camshaft Control Circuit, Bank1, Open
P1529	Intake Camshaft Control Circuit, Short to B+
P1530	Intake Camshaft Control Circuit, Short to ground
P1531	Intake Camshaft Control Circuit, open
P1533	Intake Camshaft Control Circuit, Bank2, Electrical Malfunction
P1534	Intake Camshaft Control Circuit, Bank2, Short to B+
P1535	Intake Camshaft Control Circuit, Bank2, Short to Ground
P1536	Intake Camshaft Control Circuit, Bank2, Open
P1537	Engine Shutoff Solenoid, Malfunction
P1538	Engine Shutoff Solenoid, Open/Short to Ground
P1539	Clutch Vacuum Vent Valve Switch, Incorrect signal
P1540	Vehicle Speed Sensor, High Input
P1541	Fuel Pump Relay Circuit, Open
P1542	Throttle Actuation Potentiometer, Range/Performance
P1543	Throttle Actuation Potentiometer, Signal too Low
P1544	Throttle Actuation Potentiometer, Signal too High
P1545	Throttle Position Control, Malfunction
P1546	Boost Pressure Control Valve, Short to B+

VW / AUDI / SKODA / SEAT

P1547	Boost Pressure Control Valve, Short to Ground
P1548	Boost Pressure Control Valve, Open
P1549	Boost Pressure Control Valve, Open/Short to Ground
P1550	Charge Pressure, Deviation
P1551	Barometric Pressure Sensor Circuit, Short to B+
P1552	Barometric Pressure Sensor Circuit, Open/Short to Ground
P1553	Barometric/manifold pressure signal, ratio out of range
P1554	Idle Speed Control Throttle Position, missing adaptation conditions
P1555	Charge Pressure, Upper Limit Exceeded
P1556	Charge Pressure Control, Negative Deviation
P1557	Charge Pressure Contr., Positive Deviation
P1558	Throttle Actuator, Electrical Malfunction
P1559	Idle Speed Control Throttle Position, Adaptation Malfunction
P1560	Maximum Engine Speed Exceeded
P1561	Quantity Adjuster, Deviation
P1562	Quantity Adjuster, Upper Limit Attained
P1563	Quantity Adjuster, Lower Limit Attained
P1564	Idle Speed Control Throttle Position, Low Voltage During Adaptation
P1565	Idle Speed Control Throttle Position, lower limit not attained
P1566	Load signal from A/C compressor, range/Performance
P1567	Load signal from A/C compressor, no signal
P1568	Idle Speed Control Throttle Position, mechanical Malfunction
P1569	Cruise control switch, Incorrect signal
P1570	Control Unit Locked
P1571	Left Eng. Mount Solenoid Valve, Short to B+

VW / AUDI / SKODA / SEAT

P1572	Left Eng. Mount Solenoid Valve, Short to Ground
P1573	Left Eng. Mount Solenoid Valve, Open circuit
P1574	Left Eng. Mount Solenoid Valve, Electrical fault in circuit
P1575	Right Eng. Mount Solenoid Valve, Short to B+
P1576	Right Eng. Mount Solenoid Valve, Short to ground
P1577	Right Eng. Mount Solenoid Valve, Open circuit
P1578	Right Eng. Mount Solenoid Valve, Electrical fault in circuit
P1579	Idle Speed Control Throttle Position, adaptation not started
P1580	Throttle Actuator B1, Malfunction
P1581	Idle Speed Control Throttle Position, adaptation not carried out
P1582	Idle Adaptation at Limit
P1583	Transmission mount valves, Short to B+
P1584	Transmission mount valves, Short to Ground
P1585	Transmission mount valves, Open circuit
P1586	Engine mount solenoid valves, Short to B+
P1587	Engine mount solenoid valves, Short to Ground
P1588	Engine mount solenoid valves, Open circuit
P1600	Power Supply (B+) Terminal 15, Low Voltage
P1602	Power Supply (B+) Terminal 30, Low Voltage
P1603	Internal Control Module, Self-Check
P1604	Internal Control Module, Driver Error
P1605	Rough Road/Acceleration Sensor, Electrical Malfunction
P1606	Rough Road Spec Engine Torque ABS-ECU, Electrical Malfunction
P1607	Vehicle speed signal, Error message from instrument cluster
P1608	Steering angle signal, error message from steering angle sensor

VW / AUDI / SKODA / SEAT

P1609	Crash shut down activated
P1611	MIL Call-up Circuit /Transmission Control Module, Short to Ground
P1612	Electronic Control Module, Incorrect Coding
P1613	MIL Call-up Circuit, Open/Short to B+
P1614	MIL Call-up Circuit /Transmission Control Module, Range/Performance
P1615	Engine Oil Temperature Sensor Circuit, range/Performance
P1616	Glow Plug/Heater Indicator Circuit, Short to B+
P1617	Glow Plug/Heater Indicator Circuit, Open/Short to Ground
P1618	Glow Plug/Heater Relay Circuit, Short to B+
P1619	Glow Plug/Heater Relay Circuit, Open/Short to Ground
P1620	engine coolant temperature signal, open/short to B+
P1621	Engine coolant temperature signal, short to Ground
P1622	engine coolant temperature signal, range/Performance
P1623	Data Bus Powertrain, No Communication
P1624	MIL Request Signal active
P1625	CAN-Bus, Unplausible Message from Transmission Control
P1626	CAN-Bus, Missing Message from Transmission Control
P1627	Data-Bus Powertrain, missing message from fuel injection pump
P1628	Data-Bus Powertrain, missing message from steering sensor
P1629	Data-Bus Powertrain, missing message from distance control
P1630	Acceleration Pedal Position Sensor 1, Signal too Low
P1631	Acceleration Pedal Position Sensor 1, Signal too High
P1632	Acceleration Pedal Position Sensor 1, Power Supply Malfunction
P1633	Acceleration Pedal Position Sensor 2, Signal too Low
P1634	Acceleration Pedal Position Sensor 2, Signal too High

VW / AUDI / SKODA / SEAT

P1635	Data Bus Powertrain, missing message from air condition control
P1636	Data Bus Powertrain, missing message from Airbag control
P1637	Data Bus Powertrain, missing message from central electronic control
P1638	Data Bus Powertrain, missing message from clutch control
P1639	Acceleration Pedal Position Sensor 1+2, Range/Performance
P1640	Internal Control Module (EEPROM), Error
P1641	Please check DTC Memory of Air Condition ECU
P1642	Please check DTC Memory of Airbag ECU
P1643	Please check DTC Memory of central ECU
P1644	Please check DTC Memory of clutch ECU
P1645	Data Bus Powertrain, missing message from all wheel drive control
P1646	Please check DTC Memory of all wheel drive ECU
P1647	Please check coding of ECUs in, Data Bus Powertrain
P1648	Data Bus Powertrain, defect
P1649	Data Bus Powertrain, missing message from break ECU
P1650	Data Bus Powertrain, missing message from instrument panel ECU
P1651	Data Bus Powertrain, missing messages
P1652	Please check DTC Memory of transmission ECU
P1653	Please check DTC Memory of break ECU
P1654	Please check DTC Memory of control panel ECU
P1655	Please check DTC Memory of distance control ECU
P1656	AC clutch relays circuit, short to Ground
P1657	AC clutch relays circuit, short to B+
P1658	Data-Bus Powertrain, range/performance from distance control.
P1676	Drive by Wire-MIL Circuit, Electrical Malfunction

VW / AUDI / SKODA / SEAT

P1677	Drive by Wire-MIL Circuit, Short to B+
P1678	Drive by Wire-MIL Circuit, Short to Ground
P1679	Drive by Wire-MIL Circuit, Open
P1681	Control Unit Programming, Programming not finished
P1684	Control Unit Programming, Communication Error
P1686	Control Unit Error, Programming Error
P1690	Malfunction Indication Light, Malfunction
P1691	Malfunction Indication Light, Open
P1692	Malfunction Indication Light, Short to Ground
P1693	Malfunction Indication Light, Short to B+
P1694	Malfunction Indication Light, Open/Short to Ground
P1704	Kick Down Switch, Malfunction
P1711	Wheel Speed Signal 1, Range/Performance
P1716	Wheel Speed Signal 2, Range/Performance
P1721	Wheel Speed Signal 3, Range/Performance
P1723	Starter Interlock Circuit, Open
P1724	Starter Interlock Circuit, Short to Ground
P1726	Wheel Speed Signal 4, Range/Performance
P1728	Different Wheel Speed Signals, Range/Performance
P1729	Starter Interlock Circuit, Short to B+
P1733	Tiptronic Switch Down Circuit, Short to Ground
P1739	Tiptronic Switch up Circuit, Short to Ground
P1741	Clutch pressure adaptation, adaptation at Limit
P1742	Clutch torque adaptation, adaptation at Limit
P1743	Clutch slip control, signal too high

VW / AUDI / SKODA / SEAT

P1744	Tiptronic Switch Recognition Circuit, Short to Ground
P1745	Transmission Control Unit Relay, Short to B+
P1746	Transmission Control Unit Relay, Malfunction
P1747	Transmission Control Unit Relay, Open/Short to Ground
P1748	Transmission Control Unit, Self-Check
P1749	Transmission Control Unit, Incorrect Coding
P1750	Power Supply Voltage, Low Voltage
P1751	Power Supply Voltage, High Voltage
P1752	Power Supply, Malfunction
P1760	Shift Lock, Malfunction
P1761	Shift Lock, Short to Ground
P1762	Shift Lock, Short to B+
P1763	Shift Lock, Open
P1765	Hydraulic Pressure Sensor 2, adaptation at Limit
P1766	Throttle Angle Signal, Stuck Off
P1767	Throttle Angle Signal, Stuck On
P1768	Hydraulic Pressure Sensor 2, Too High
P1769	Hydraulic Pressure Sensor 2, Too Low
P1770	Load Signal, Range/Performance
P1771	Load Signal, Stuck Off
P1772	Load Signal, Stuck On
P1773	Hydraulic Pressure Sensor 1, Too High
P1774	Hydraulic Pressure Sensor 1, Too Low
P1775	Hydraulic Pressure Sensor 1, Adaptation at Limit
P1778	Solenoid EV7, Electrical Malfunction

VW / AUDI / SKODA / SEAT

P1781	Engine Torque Reduction, Open/Short to Ground
P1782	Engine Torque Reduction, Short to B+
P1784	Shift up/down Wire, Open/Short to Ground
P1785	Shift up/down Wire, Short to B+
P1786	Reversing Light Circuit, Open
P1787	Reversing Light Circuit, Short to Ground
P1788	Reversing Light Circuit, Short to B+
P1789	Idle Speed Intervention Circuit, Error Message from Engine Control
P1790	Transmission Range Display Circuit, Open
P1791	Transmission Range Display Circuit, Short to Ground
P1792	Transmission Range Display Circuit, Short to B+
P1793	Output Speed Sensor 2 Circuit, no signal
P1795	Vehicle Speed Signal Circuit, Open
P1796	Vehicle Speed Signal Circuit, Short to Ground
P1797	Vehicle Speed Signal Circuit, Short to B+
P1798	Output Speed Sensor 2 Circuit, Range/Performance
P1799	Output Speed Sensor 2 Circuit, RPM too High
P1813	Pressure Control Solenoid 1, Electrical
P1814	Pressure Control Solenoid 1, Open/Short to Ground
P1815	Pressure Control Solenoid 1, Short to B+
P1818	Pressure Control Solenoid 2, Electrical
P1819	Pressure Control Solenoid 2, Open/Short to Ground
P1820	Pressure Control Solenoid 2, Short to B+
P1823	Pressure Control Solenoid 3, Electrical
P1824	Pressure Control Solenoid 3, Open/Short to Ground

VW / AUDI / SKODA / SEAT

P1825	Pressure Control Solenoid 3, Short to B+
P1828	Pressure Control Solenoid 4, Electrical
P1829	Pressure Control Solenoid 4, Open/Short to Ground
P1830	Pressure Control Solenoid 4, Short to B+
P1834	Pressure Control Solenoid 5, Open/Short to Ground
P1835	Pressure Control Solenoid 5, Short to B+
P1841	Engine/Transmission control, do not match
P1842	Please check DTC Memory of instrument panel ECU
P1843	Please check DTC Memory of distance control ECU
P1844	Please check DTC Memory of central electric control ECU
P1847	Please check DTC Memory of brake system ECU
P1848	Please check DTC Memory of engine ECU
P1849	Please check DTC Memory of transmission ECU
P1850	CAN-Bus, Missing Message from Engine Control
P1851	CAN-Bus, Missing Message from Brake Control
P1852	CAN-Bus, Unplausible Message from Engine Control
P1853	CAN-Bus, Unplausible Message from Brake Control
P1854	CAN-Bus, Hardware Defective
P1855	CAN-Bus, Software version Control
P1856	Throttle/Pedal Position Sensor A Circuit, Error Message from Engine Control
P1857	Load Signal, Error Message from Engine Control
P1858	Engine Speed Input Circuit, Error Message from Engine Control
P1859	Brake Switch Circuit, Error Message from Engine Control
P1860	Kick Down Switch, Error Message from Engine Control
P1861	Throttle Position (TP) sensor, Error Message from ECM

OBD II FAULT CODES

VW / AUDI / SKODA / SEAT

P1862	Data Bus Powertrain, missing message from instrument panel ECU
P1863	Data Bus Powertrain, Missing Message from St. Angle Sensor
P1864	Data Bus Powertrain, Missing message from ADR control module
P1865	Data Bus Powertrain, Missing message from central electronics
P1866	Data Bus Powertrain, Missing messages

NOTES

CM 11-9-06
TC 1-11-07
ST 3-15-07
OS 5-17-07
AC 7-19-07
PL 9-20-07
ET 11-28-07
WH 1-28-07

WH 1-31-08 KP

DISCARD